World Hunger

TEN MYTHS

Fourth Edition • Thoroughly Revised and Updated

WORLD HUNGER

Ten Myths

Frances Moore Lappé
& Joseph Collins

Institute for Food and Development Policy

To order additional copies of this book:
1 to 6 copies $2.75
7 to 49 copies $1.95
50 or more copies............... $1.65

Add 10% for postage and handling costs.

Make checks payable to Institute for Food and Development Policy, 2588 Mission Street, San Francisco, California 94110 U. S. A.

ISBN: 0-935028-00-5

fourth edition
second printing, May 1980

Design, Barbara Garza; production, Dina Redman; typesetting, Sherrell Graphics; printing, Riteway-Haluska. The text for this book was set in 10 point Palatino.

Contents

For us, learning had to begin with unlearning. Here we want to share ten pervasive myths that prevented us from grasping how hunger is generated and how some countries are attacking the root causes of hunger to achieve food security.

For the last several years we have grappled with the question "why hunger?" Analyses that call for increasing or improving present development assistance or for reducing our consumption so that the hungry might eat left us with gnawing doubts. We probed and probed. We finally had to conclude that:

- Every country in the world has the resources necessary for its people to free themselves from hunger.
- Food security cannot be measured in grain reserves or production figures.
- A nation's per capita food production can increase and yet more people can be more hungry.
- Official foreign development assistance can contribute to the increased impoverishment of the very groups it claims to be helping most.

We agonized over the logical consequences of what we were learning that seemed to put us in conflict with positions we previously had supported. But eventually we came to an understanding that provides direction and energy instead of paralyzing us with guilt, fear, or despair.

Men stack wheat for storage in Damota, Ethiopia. *World Bank photo by Ray Witlin.*

MYTH
ONE

People are hungry because of scarcity.

Hunger exists in the face of plenty; therein lies the outrage. Right now the earth is producing more than enough to nourish every human being, both on a global level and even within the very countries we all associate with hunger and starvation.

Measured globally, there is more than enough to feed everyone. Considering only grain, enough is produced to provide everyone with ample protein and more than 3000 calories a day, about the caloric intake of the average American. (A third or more of this grain is now fed to livestock.) And this 3000 calorie estimate does not include many other foods—beans, root crops, fruits, nuts, vegetables, and grass-fed meats.[1]

But global estimates mean little except to dispel the widespread notion that we have reached the earth's limits. What really explodes the myth that scarcity is the cause of hunger is the fact that enough food is being produced even in countries where so many are forced to go hungry.

In India, while millions starve, soldiers patrol the government's 16 million tons of "surplus" grain.[2] In the Sahelian countries of West Africa even during the much-publicized drought and famine of the early seventies, surveys by the United Nations Food and Agriculture Organization, squelched by displeased aid-seeking governments, documented that each Sahelian country, with the possible exception of mineral-rich Mauritania, actually produced enough grain to feed its total population.[3] In Mexico, where at least 80 percent of the children in the rural areas are undernourished, livestock (much of it raised for export to the United States) consume more basic grains than the country's entire rural population.[4]

In Bangladesh, one of the world's most densely populated countries, enough grain is produced to provide, theoretically, each person with more than 2600 calories a day.[5] Yet over half the families in Bangladesh daily consume less than 1500 calories per person, the bare minimum necessary.[6] Following the 1974 floods, millions in Bangladesh perished. But they did not die because of scarcity. One Bangladeshi describes what happened in her village: "A lot of people died of starvation here. The rich farmers were holding rice and not letting any of the poor peasants see ..." Asked whether there was enough food in the village, she replied, "There may not have been a lot of food, but if it had been shared, no one would have died."[7]

Nor should we ever forget that in the United States millions have not enough to eat. Who would argue it is because there is not enough food produced?

Hunger is real; scarcity is not.

Cattle Drawn cart on north-south highway in Brazil. *World Bank photo by Tomas Sennett.*

MYTH
TWO

Hunger results from overpopulation: There are just too many people for food-producing resources to sustain.

If "too many people" caused hunger, we would expect to find the most hunger in countries having the most people for each cropped acre. Yet we find no such pattern. Compare China and India, for example. China has merely half the cultivated acreage for each person that India has.[8] Yet in only 20 years the Chinese people succeeded in eliminating visible hunger while so many Indians still go hungry.

We also find countries with comparatively large amounts of agricultural land per person that, even so, have some of the most severe and chronic hunger in the world. While severe hunger is a daily reality for most Bolivians, their country has well over one-half acre of cultivated land per person, significantly more than in France, and potentially ten cultivable acres per person.[9] Brazil has more cultivated acreage per person than the United States, yet in recent years the percent of the people undernourished has increased from 45 percent to 72 percent.[10] Mexico, where most of the rural population suffers from undernourishment, has more cultivated land per person than Cuba, where now no one goes hungry.[11]

In Africa, south of the Sahara, where we find some of the worst and most chronic hunger in the world, there are almost two and one-half *cultivated* acres per person,[12] more than in the United States or the Soviet Union and six to eight times more than in China.

Certainly there are a few countries in Latin America with both a relatively high population density and widespread hunger — countries like Haiti and the Dominican Republic. Haiti and the Dominican Republic, nonetheless, have just slightly less cultivated land per person and a much longer growing season than Italy.[13] This calculation does not even include the considerable additional area uncultivated in these two Caribbean countries many agronomists agree is good agricultural land. This land is officially classified as "permanent pasture" simply because the well-off owners choose to graze livestock on it.

The tremendous and needless underutilization of food producing resources allows us only to conclude that so-called overpopulation is not the cause of hunger. Of all the earth's cultivable land, less than half is now being cropped.[14] In most underdeveloped countries, average grain yields are one half what they are in the industrial countries.[15] And much land, presently harvested only once yearly, could provide two or even more harvests. Bangladesh,[16] for instance, has excellent conditions for rice cultivation — rich alluvial soils, tropical sun and abundant rainfall that could readily be controlled for irrigation. Yet most of the land is planted with rice only once a year and the average yields are only one-third of those of the industrial countries and one-sixth of those proven possible in Bangladesh.[17]

Such underutilization of food-producing resources characterizes every society where, as in Bangladesh, land and the credit and marketing system are controlled by a few and those who work the land do not have effective control over it. The real barriers to greater production are not physical but political and economic — as we detail in our response to Myth Seven.

The fact that the myth that hunger is caused by "overpopulation" is so widespread is in itself revealing. It says a lot about how we all are conditioned to regard people. Are we not made to think of people as an economic liability when, in reality, all the wealth of any country begins with people—with human labor? The economic security of a nation depends not so much on rich natural resources as on how effectively its people can be motivated and their labor utilized.

While Americans think of the Third World in terms of excessive numbers of people swamping agriculture in search of work, the facts reveal that their labor could well be effectively used. Agriculturally successful countries like Japan have twice the number of workers per acre found in countries like India and the Philippines.[18] According to a World Bank study,[19] if countries like India attained Japan's level of labor intensity (two workers per hectare) their agriculture could absorb all the labor force expected by 1985. Many economists, moreover, have argued that certain countries in Africa are underpopulated in view of the sizeable labor force needed to bring into production untapped agricultural resources. In other words, people appear as a liability only in a certain kind of economic system. People are not born marginal.

"Marginal people," hunger itself, and high birth rates, all three turn out to be *symptoms*. They are symptoms of the same disease— the insecurity and poverty of the majority resulting from the monopolizing of productive assets by a few.

High birth rates are often people's defensive reaction to such a system: people need to have many children in order to provide laborers to augment meager family income. Many children are also needed to provide old-age security and to compensate for the high infant death rate, the result of inadequate nutrition and health care. Moreover, high birth rates can reflect the social powerlessness of women, which is exacerbated by poverty. In most cases, the greater the poverty, the greater the oppression of women. Birth rates do not fall until women gain control over reproductive decisions, a process that cannot occur in isolation from both men and women achieving economic self-determination.

No one should discount the long-term consequences of rapid population growth. High population densities can make more difficult the tasks of social and economic restructuring necessary to eliminate hunger. The error, however, is to transform the problem of population—a symptom and exacerbating factor—into the cause of hunger. This is not semantic squabble. Getting at the solution to any problem hinges on how well one can pinpoint its root cause. The root cause of hunger has to do with the relationships of people to each other and to their control over resources. As long as people think the fundamental cause is elsewhere, the hungry will in fact be made hungrier. Indeed, to attack high birth rates without attacking the causes of poverty and the powerlessness of women is fruitless. It is a tragic diversion our planet cannot afford.

Rice threshing combine with Liberian operators and U.S. technician. *Agency for International Development.*

MYTH
THREE

To solve the problem of hunger the top priority must be on growing more food.

Food production per person in underdeveloped countries as a whole is above the level of 20 years ago.[20] Yet in some of the most productively successful countries, there is more hunger than ever. How can we explain the apparent contradiction of more food per person and yet more hunger?

Wherever we find unlimited private control over resources and individual producer pitted against individual producer, we find emerging extreme inequalities in control over resources. In such systems, those with even the slightest edge are able to expand at the expense of the others. One measure of inequality in control is the fact that, according to a United Nations survey of 83 countries, approximately three percent of all landlords have come to control almost 80 percent of the land.[21] Another measure of inequality is the access to credit. In most countries only five to 20 percent of all producers have access to institutional credit.[22] The rest must turn to landlords and moneylenders at usurious rates running as high as 200 percent.

When a new agricultural technology—such as hybrid seeds that yield more in response to irrigation, fertilizers and pesticides— is introduced into a social system shot through with such power inequalities, it inevitably benefits only those who already possess land, money, credit "worthiness," or political influence or some combination of these. This is simply a social fact.

Indeed, it is now well documented:[23] strategies that have avoided the issue of who controls productive assets, attempting only to get more produced, have set into motion a catastrophic chain of events that actually worsens the plight of the poor majority. The potential productivity represented by the new technology attracts a new class of "farmers"—moneylenders, military officers, bureaucrats, city-based speculators and foreign corporations—who rush in and buy up land. Land values soar—up, for instance, three to fivefold in only a few years in the "Green Revolution" areas of India. As land values rise, so do rents, pushing tenants and sharecroppers into the ranks of the landless. Seeing new profit possibilities, landlords evict their tenants and cultivate the land themselves with the new agricultural machinery. The percentage of rural workforce that is landless has doubled in India (now over one-third) since the introduction of Green Revolution innovations. In northwest Mexico, the birthplace of the Green Revolution, the average farm size has jumped from 200 to 2000 acres with over three-quarters of the rural labor force now deprived of any land at all.[24]

And, while more landless are created by the expansion of the better-off growers, fewer jobs are available to them. The large commercial operators mechanize to maximize profits and avoid "labor management problems." With mechanization in the agricultural boom areas of northwest Mexico, the average number of days of employment for each laborer fell from 190 to 100.[25]

In country after country where agricultural resources are still regarded only as a source of individual wealth, the narrow drive to increase production totals ends up excluding the majority of rural people from control over the production process. And, we have found, *to be cut out of production is to be cut out of consumption.* As a 36¢ a day agricultural laborer in Bihar, India, observes: "If you don't own any land, you never get enough to eat, even if the land is producing well."[26]

Take, for example, rice in the Thanjavur district in southern India. There, as a result of the introduction of new technologies, the rice yields are three times the national Indian average. Yet those who do the work are increasingly desperate. As land concentration increases, two-thirds of the agricultural laborers have become virtually landless. As much as 50 percent of the rice produced in Thanjavur leaves the district for other districts where people can pay more—or even for export. And the main protein source for the Dalit agricultural laborers who work the Thanjavur rice fields is *rats* that in turn live off the stored rice crop.[27]

Empirical studies recently prepared for the International Labor Organization[28] document that in the very Asian countries— Pakistan, India, Sri Lanka, Malaysia, the Philippines and Indonesia—where the focus has merely been on getting total food production increased and where food production per capita has in fact risen, the rural poor are absolutely worse off than before. The study concludes that "the increase in poverty has been associated not with a fall but with a rise in cereal production per head, the main component of the diet of the poor." These six countries account for two-thirds of the rural population of the non-socialist Third World. In-depth investigations by the United Nations Research Institute for Social Development (UNRISD) of the impact of Green Revolution techniques in 24 different underdeveloped countries have confirmed this consistent pattern—a decline in well-being for much of the rural majority even as agricultural production bounds ahead.[29]

This process of cutting increasing numbers of rural people out of control over production is not confined to Third World countries. The same forces are operating in the United States. Here new agricultural technologies also abet the shakeout process as in the Third World.

Designed to be profitable only for the large operation, new machinery can cut production costs. But those who do not control enough land to make a new technology pay find it hard to compete with those who do. Witness the fate of small tomato growers in California. In the early 1960's tax-funded agricultural research developed tomato harvesters so large that only a small minority of the growers had enough land and capital to take advantage of them. While these large operators reduced their labor costs and prospered, 3400 out of the 4000 growers were driven out of business in only eight years.[30] (And what we get is the hardly recognizable, unbruisable tomato bred for machine picking. Nor have the cost-cutting gains of the new technology been passed on to the consumer.)

Over the past 25 years the Green Revolution in American agriculture has meant the loss of 1900 farms each week.[31] Black farmers, among the poorest farmers in the United States, are now losing almost 10,000 acres per week. At this rate, Blacks will be landless by 1983.[32] More than half of America's farmland is now owned by absentee landlords.[33] In California 45 corporations have taken control of 30 percent of the state's best farmland.[34] Over half of the nation's farmland is now in the control of only 5.5 percent of all farmowners.[35]

Increasingly heavy farm debt—greater than ever before—threatens to ruin yet more farmers. A full one-half of the net income of U.S. farmers now goes out in interest payments on a $120 billion debt.[36] Such a heavy debt burden means great vulnerability—especially for the smaller operator. As one U.S. farmer explained to us, "When the prices we get drop below our costs, a big operator can write off his losses and plan for next year. But the small guy is done for. He has to get out."

Farmers are forced into such debt to buy ever higher priced farm inputs. Keep in mind that approximately 80 percent of the gross returns farmers get from selling their crops goes for production costs like fertilizers and machinery.[37] In the U.S. and Canada two corporate giants, John Deere and International Harvester, control half of the tractor sales and two-thirds of the sales of combines.[38] Such monopoly control by a handful of machinery corporations, according to a 1972 Federal Trade Commission investigation, resulted in a single year in $251 million in overcharges to American farmers.[39]

Our point in addressing the "myth of the production solution" is not to disparage the role of technology in development. The issue is not pro or con technology. The issue is: technology in whose interest? Even the so-called appropriate small-scale technology can further undermine the position of the poor in a society structured against them.

Consider, for example, biogasification, a relatively simple method of fermenting organic raw materials such as crop residues and manure to produce both fuel and fertilizer. A small-scale biogas plant can be built from local materials. But even this apparently beneficial technology has created greater problems for the poorer groups in a country like India. First, even the smallest plants require a significant investment and the dung from two cows. Thus only well-off farmers who have cows and some capital to invest come to control the biogas. Furthermore, the dung, which had been free, now has cash value. In areas where biogas plants operate, landless laborers can no longer find it on the road and use it for fuel. And since the landless and the other poor villagers are in no position to buy biogas, they end up with no fuel at all.[40]

Before even a step in the right direction can be made, we must come to understand that a strategy emphasizing increased production while ignoring who is in control of that production is not a neutral strategy. It does not "buy us time"—that is, feed people while the more difficult social questions of control can be addressed. No. Such a strategy is taking us backward, itself creating ever greater impoverishment and hunger.

Woman spraying pesticide on rice field in Taiwan. *Kay Chernush*

MYTH
FOUR

Even if there is enough food today, more people will require increased food production and that can come only at the expense of the ecological integrity of our food-producing resources. Pesticide use, for instance, will have to be stepped up even if the risks are great. And farming will have to be pushed onto marginal lands at the risk of irreparable erosion.

We too found ourselves wondering whether a legitimate and urgent need for more food will not require injecting ever more pesticides into our environment. To grow more food, won't we have to accept the environmental and health risks of these deadly chemicals?

To answer that question we first had to ask: just how pesticide-dependent is the world's current food production? In the United States about 1.2 billion pounds, a whopping six pounds for every American and 30 percent of the world's total, are dumped into the environment every year. Surely, we thought, such a staggering figure means that practically every acre of U.S. farmland is dosed with deadly poisons. U.S. food abundance appeared to us as the plus that comes from such a big minus. The facts, however, proved us wrong.

Fact One: About one-third of the pesticides in the United States are used not on farmland but on golf courses, parks and lawns.[41]

Fact Two: Only about five percent of the nation's crop and pasture-land is treated with insecticides, 15 percent with weed-killers, and 0.5 percent with fungicides.[42]

Fact Three: Over half of all insecticides applied in United States agriculture are used on nonfood crops. Cotton alone receives almost half (47 percent) of all insecticides used. It should be noted that, even then, half of the country's total cotton acreage receives no insecticide treatment at all.[43]

Fact Four: Thirty years ago American farmers used 50 million pounds of pesticides and lost 7 percent of their crop before harvest. Today, farmers use twelve times more pesticides, yet the percentage of the crop lost before harvest has almost doubled.[44]

Fact Five: Even if all pesticides were eliminated, crop loss due to pests (insects, pathogens, weeds, mammals, and birds) would rise only about seven percentage points, from 33.6 to 40.7 percent.[45] Such an increase does not take into account the possible use of alternatives to chemicals.

And what about the underdeveloped countries? Do pesticides there help produce food for hungry people?

In underdeveloped countries most pesticides are used for export crops, prinicipally cotton, and to a lesser extent for export fruits and vegetables planted uniformly in vast expanses, a condition known to exacerbate pest problems.[46] The quantities of pesticides injected into the world's environment therefore have little to do with the hungry's food needs.

The alternatives to chemical pesticides—crop rotation, mixed cropping, mulching, hand weeding, hoeing, collection of pest eggs, manipulation of natural predators, and so on—are numerous and proven effective. The first step, however, is spraying only in response to need. Cotton growers in Graham County, Arizona, found they could reduce pest damage tenfold and pest control costs fivefold by spraying only in response to a specific outbreak rather than the blind, scheduled spraying recommended by pesticide manufacturers.[47] The Chinese have minimized pesticide use through a nationwide early warning system.[48] In Shao-tung county in Honan province, 10,000 youths make up watch teams that patrol the fields and report any sign of pest damage. Appropriately called the "barefoot doctors of agriculture," they have succeeded in reducing the damage of wheat rust and rice borer to less than one percent and in bringing locust invasions under control.

All these alternatives would increase the numbers who could be productively employed in agriculture, thus taking advantage of a country's most underutilized resource while reducing dependence on imported inputs. But the alternatives require the motivation of farmers who have the security of individual or group tenure over the land they work. Clearly, environmentally safe techniques for pest control will never be developed and employed widely as long as the problem is seen as merely a technical one to be solved by profit-maximizing chemical corporations.

Is the need for food for a growing population the real pressure forcing people to farm marginal lands that are easily destroyed? We investigated many of the most likely cases around the world.

Haiti offers a shocking picture of environmental destruction. The majority of the peasants ravage the once-green mountain slopes in a desperate effort to grow food. Has food production for Haitians used up every safely cultivated acre so that only the mountain slopes are left? No. These peasants seeking to farm the fragile slopes can only be seen as exiles from their birthright—some of the world's richest agricultural land. The rich valley lands are in the control of a handful of elites (and their American partners) whose concern is not food but dollars to pay for an imported lifestyle. These fertile lands are thus made to produce largely low nutrition and feed crops (sugar, coffee, cocoa, alfalfa for cattle) exclusively for export. In the early 1970's some Texas-based operators began to fly cattle into Haiti for grazing and re-export to the American institutional and fast food market.

In Colombia a World Bank study[50] concluded that "large numbers of farm families . . . try to eke out an existence on too little land, often on slopes of . . . 45 degrees or more. As a result, they exploit the land very severely, adding to erosion and other problems, and even so are not able to make a decent living."

Overpopulation? No. Colombia's good level land is in the hands of absentee landlords who keep it idle or use it to graze cattle, raise animal feed and even flowers for export to the United States.

In Africa, large tracts of land perfectly suitable for permanent crops such as grazing grasses and fruit or nut trees have been torn up for planting cotton and peanuts for export. In parts of Senegal the peanut monoculture imposed on the peasant farmers, first by the French colonial administrators and now by the taxation and other programs of elite governments, has devastated the soils.

The Amazon is rapidly being de-forested. Is it because of the pressure of Brazil's growing population? Brazil's ratio of cultivable land to people is slightly better than that of the United States (and the Amazon forest is not counted as cultivable). The Amazon forest, then, is being destroyed not because of a shortage of farmland. Even though agronomists have warned that tropical forest soils are not suited to permanent cropping, the military dictatorship is promising the landless people "new frontiers" in the Amazon basin. This is one way of deflecting popular demands for land redistribution and thereby protecting the largest estates, controlling 43 percent of Brazil's farmland. But in reality, only a few thousand peasants have received any land. At the same time, multinational corporations like Anderson Clayton, Goodyear, Volkswagen, Nestlé, Liquigas, Borden, Mitsubishi, and multi-billionaire Daniel Ludwig's Universe Tank Ship Co. get massive government subsidies to bulldoze hundreds of millions of acres to produce beef, rice and wood for upper income domestic and foreign markets.[51] Scientists disagree over only *how* monumental the devastation to the planet's environment will be.

In the United States we find a pattern of soil destruction not unlike what we have discovered in underdeveloped countries. The accelerated drive to increase agricultural exports, begun in the early 1970's, is taking its toll on our nation's soil and our longterm food security. The intense pressure to increase U.S. production for export to earn foreign exchange has brought more erosion-prone soils into production, has decreased or eliminated fallow periods that regenerate the soil and has led to the continuous planting of corn or other row crops that expose the soil to erosion, as opposed to crops such as hay that make the soil more erosion resistant. More than half of the nearly 10 million acres of former pastures, woodlands, and idle fields converted to crops in late 1973 and early 1974 received inadequate soil conservation treatment. In the southern part of the Great Plains, the annual topsoil loss on 50,000 acres of newly planted land now amounts to 15 to 125 tons per acre.[52]

Another study concludes that soil loss due to erosion in western Iowa is up 22 percent because of current U.S. farm policy to increase agricultural production for export.[53] According to a Soil Conservation Service official in Iowa, that state is now losing an average of ten tons of topsoil per acre each year. Expressed another way, on much of the sloping land in Iowa, a farmer is losing two bushels of topsoil for every one bushel of corn produced![54] At this rate, all of the topsoil in Iowa will be gone within less than a century.

Moreover, now that agriculture is the latest speculative industry, new irrigation technology is spreading to marginal soils. Center-pivot irrigation makes possible the cultivation of sandy, marginal soils not possible with other types of irrigation. But sandy soils are erosion-prone and leach soil nutrients into the ground, causing pollution of waterways. In addition, center-pivot irrigation, a pushbutton sprinkler system of two rotating pipes, each one-quarter mile long, cannot accomodate trees. The trees must go. And indeed they do. Precious "shelterbelts," rows of trees planted by conservation-conscious farmers years ago, are now being pulled up to make way for the center-pivots.[55]

Nor should we be led to think that this destruction of soil resources is due to pressing U.S. or world food needs: most of U.S. agricultural exports go to other industrial countries and about half of our agricultural exports go to feed livestock.

It is not, then, the growing population that threatens to destroy the environment either here or abroad, but other forces: land monopolizers that export nonfood and luxury crops, forcing the rural majority to abuse marginal lands; colonial patterns of cash cropping that are reinforced by elites today; and a system that promotes the utilization of food-producing resources simply according to profit-seeking criteria. Cutting the world's population in half tomorrow would not stop any of these forces.

Scene in Managua, Nicaragua after the 1972 earthquake. *Agency for International Development.*

MYTH
FIVE

Hunger is a contest between the Rich World and the Poor World.

Terms like "poor world" and "hungry world" make us think of uniformly hungry masses. They hide the reality of stratified societies in both underdeveloped countries and industrially developed countries like the United States. Poverty and hunger afflict the lower rungs in both. Terms like "hungry world" make hunger into a place—and usually a place far away. Rather than being a result of a social process, hunger becomes a static fact, a geographic given.

Worse still, the all-inclusiveness of these labels leads us to believe that everyone living in a country has a common interest in eliminating hunger. Thus, we look at an underdeveloped country and assume its government officials represent the hungry majority. We then are tempted to believe that concessions to these governments, e.g., lower tariffs on their exports, or increased foreign investment, automatically represent progress for the hungry. In fact, the "progress" may be only for the elites and their partners, multinational corporations.

Moreover, the "rich world" versus "poor world" scenario makes the hungry appear as a threat to the well-being of the majority in the industrially developed countries. In truth, however, hunger will never be addressed until average citizens in countries like the United States see that the hungry abroad are their allies, not their enemies. For the interests of the majority of Americans are linked with those of the hungry majority in the underdeveloped countries through a common threat: the tightening of control over food—both within countries and on a global scale.

As we pointed out in exposing Myth Three, concentrated control over food-producing resources that we can identify as the direct cause of hunger and poverty in the Third World is accelerating in the United States. But concentrated control over land and farm inputs is only one aspect. Equally important is the tightening of control over food processing and marketing. In the mid-sixties a Federal Trade Commission study estimated that fewer than 0.2 percent of all food manufacturers (or 50 out of almost 30,000 firms) had gained control over about 50 percent of all the industry's assets.[56] Since then, large companies have been gobbled up by giant companies—recently Del Monte by R.J. Reynolds and Green Giant by Pillsbury, to cite only a few. Over the last 25 years one industry conglomerate, Beatrice Foods, has bought up over 400 other companies.[57] Revealing of their strengthened market power, the top 50 firms now capture close to 90 percent of the industry's profits.[58]

Oligopoly control means oligopoly pricing. The food processing oligopolies, according to several studies, yearly overcharge American consumers $12 to $14 billion.[59] Food marketing is also highly concentrated, resulting, according to a Congressional study, in significant "monopoly overcharges." In 1974, in a sampling of just 32 cities, consumers paid $662 million more than they should have, due to the concentrated power of the supermarket chains.[60] For those one out of ten Americans who must spend 69 percent of their income on food,[61] such price gouging means under-nutrition. And as long as such oligopolies artificially inflate food prices it will be virtually impossible for family farmers ever to receive the prices they need to stay on the farm without raising consumer food costs.

The parallels between the forces of hunger faced by people in the Third World and the forces of concentrated control over *our* food, suggested here and in our response to Myth Three, are only part of what make us allies. In addition to the parallel forces of economic concentration, there are powerful and growing interconnections between their plight and ours.

For many of the oligopolistic food corporations, having become giants nationally, are now expanding their operations into underdeveloped countries. Finding production sites in underdeveloped countries where land and labor can cost as little as 10 percent of those stateside, large food processors and marketers are seeking supplies and often shifting production of high value items — vegetables, fruits, flowers, and meat — out of countries like the United States. They find ready partners in foreign elites, who, by exacerbating the impoverishment of much of the local population, have depressed the domestic market for their production.

Del Monte now exports pineapples from Kenya and the Philippines to the United States, Europe, and Japan; the House of Bud, the European affiliate of the California lettuce grower now owned by Castle and Cook ("Dole") airfreights fresh produce from Africa to Europe; and United Brands jets cut flowers from Central America to the United States. These multinational agribusiness firms are busily creating a Global Farm to serve a Global Supermarket. In the Global Supermarket food is auctioned off to the highest bidders wherever they might live. The tragic reality is that when the market rules, even America's 65 million dogs and cats can — and do — outbid the hungry people of the world. Thus, consumers in the United States unwittingly become a suction force, diverting food-producing resources in the underdeveloped countries away from meeting local needs. And increasingly the prime agricultural resources of countries like the United States will be made to produce, sometimes even under foreign control, for high income consumers abroad, notably in the oil-exporting countries.

The tightening of control over our food supply, embodied in the Global Supermarket, can also be measured by the degree of monopoly control of international trade in certain key commodities. A mere five corporations control 90 percent of all grain that is shipped across national borders.[62] The multinational corporation Unilever, known in the United States as Lever Brothers, controls 80 percent of corn oil, soy oil, peanut oil, and all other edible oils in world trade.[63] Four corporations control 90 percent of world banana trade.[64]

Since the beginning of colonial times, Third World agriculture has been viewed as a source of raw materials for the metropolitan countries. What then is different about the Global Supermarket being constructed today?

First, many of the items being exported to the industrial countries are items that had historically been grown by their own farmers. Today, for example, the United States imports from one-half to two-thirds of the principal winter and early spring vegetables, largely from Mexico.[65] Indeed, in 1977 the United States imported $13 billion in agricultural products.[66] About one-half of these agricultural imports are commodities that the United States can and does produce—meat, sugar, vegetables, tobacco, wine, and dairy products.[67] Thus U.S. farmers and food processing workers are threatened.

Second, as those in the underdeveloped countries become increasingly impoverished, they can no longer make effective market demand even on staple food items. Poor people's foods such as cassava in Thailand[68] or beans in Chile become booming exports.[69]

But do U.S. consumers benefit by the global reach of the corporate food giants? No. There is no evidence that U.S. consumers get cheaper food. Nor are foods bred for world travel more nutritious or better tasting. Who then does gain from the Global Supermarket? Only its creators. The return on equity on Third World operations are invariably higher than elsewhere, despite deliberate underreporting. Earnings for Del Monte's Philippine operations average four times those for their operations in the U.S.[70]

While U.S. citizens do not gain by the internationalization of food control embodied in the Global Supermarket, they are made, nevertheless, to underwrite its construction. Through the Overseas Private Investment Corporation, for instance, more than $3 billion dollars from the U.S. Treasury now guarantees investments abroad by private U.S. companies. Forty-one percent of OPIC insurance issued between 1974 and 1976 went to just 11 of the largest U.S. multinational corporations.[71] OPIC has insured Del Monte's pineapple processing plant in Kenya and Ralston Purina's fast food chains in Brazil. Furthermore, taxpayer money going to the Agency for International Development is loaned to the Latin American Agribusiness Development Corporation (LAAD), an investment company whose shareholders are some of the world's largest agribusiness companies, including Cargill, John Deere, Ralston Purina, Borden, and many more. To date LAAD has collaborated with local elites in Central America and the Caribbean, developing and investing in 66 projects engaged in production and export of luxury items such as fresh and frozen vegetables, cut flowers, and meat.[72]

Under the banner of food "interdependence," multinational agribusiness corporations are now creating a single global agricultural system in which they would exercise integrated control over all stages of production from farm to consumer. If they succeed, they—like the oil companies—will be able to effectively manipulate supply and prices on a worldwide basis through monopoly practices already well rehearsed on a national basis in the United States. Farmers, workers and consumers everywhere are already experiencing the costs of food monopolization in terms of rising prices, artificial shortages, and diminishing quality. Encouraged by the U.S. taxpayer's support, protected by strong U.S. military and diplomatic ties to precisely the kind of governments most favoring foreign investments, the Global Farm and Supermarket are creating the type of interdependence no one needs. "Interdependence" in a world of extreme power inequalities becomes a smokescreen for the usurpation of food resources by a few for a few.

Bales of cotton for export at Port of Santos, Brazil. *World Bank photo by Tomas Sennett*

MYTH
SIX

If countries where so many go hungry did not produce agri-cultural exports, then the land now growing for foreign consumers would nourish local people. Export agriculture, therefore, is the enemy.

Export agriculture is *not* the enemy. Export-oriented agriculture in countries where many go hungry is largely a *reflection* of the problem, not the problem itself. An export focus in countries where many go hungry reflects the impoverishment of much of the local population and the interests of the elite. Even if all agricultural exports stopped, there still would be hungry people—those who are excluded from genuine control over their country's food-producing resources.

An export focus nonetheless is an *active* force. The very success of export agriculture can further undermine the position of most of the rural population. When commodity prices go up, tenants and self-provisioning farmers are threatened with loss of their land as the big landholders expand their holdings in order to profit from the higher commodity prices. Moreover, a jump in the world price of a major export commodity can trigger overall inflation which results in less real income for the plantation worker or peasant producer. For instance, when in 1974 the world price of sugar increased several fold, the real wage of a cane cutter in the Dominican Republic actually fell to less than it was ten years earlier; a nominal increase in a cane cutter's wage did not compensate for the inflation set off by the sugar boom.[73]

Moreover, governments giving priority to agricultural exports are governments that relentlessly suppress movements for land redistribution and other democratic social reforms. Minimum wage laws for agricultural laborers are not enacted, for example, because they might make the country's exports "uncompetitive." Such governments exempt land producing for export from land reform and thereby further undercut local food production as growers shift to export crops to avoid having to sell their land. Thus, in the Philippines, in 1974-1975, 232,000 more acres were planted in sugar (and therefore exempted from land reform) than just three years earlier.[74]

Finally, export-oriented agricultural operations invariably import capital-intensive technologies, such as chemical fertilizers and pesticides, to maximize yields as well as to meet the foreign market's "beauty standards" and processing specifications. Basing an agricultural system on imported technologies helps ensure that whatever is produced will be exported to pay the import bill—a vicious circle of dependency.

In sum, where productive assets are controlled by a few, export agriculture further exacerbates the deteriorating position of the majority. Export agriculture:

— makes it possible for the local economic elite to be unconcerned about the poverty at home that greatly limits the buying power of most of the local people. Through producing for export the elite can profit anyway by finding buyers in the United States and other high-paying markets.

— provides the incentive to local and foreign elites to tighten their control over productive resources from which export profits are made and to resist firmly any attempts at redistribution of control over productive assets.

—necessitates miserable working conditions and wages. Underdeveloped countries can compete in export markets only by exploiting labor, especially women and children. Owners and export-oriented governments will stop at nothing to crush workers' efforts to organize themselves.

—throws the local population into competition with foreign consumers for the products of their own land, thus raising local prices and reducing the real income of the majority.

Contrasting two Caribbean countries—Cuba and the Dominican Republic—reveals, however, that export agriculture itself is not the real enemy. In both countries a large portion of agricultural land produces sugar and other exports. Both countries rely on agricultural exports for foreign exchange and both import significant amounts of grain. Yet today in the Dominican Republic, at least 75 percent of the people are undernourished, while in Cuba there is virtually no malnutrition.

First, the foreign exchange earned from sugar imports is controlled very differently in the two countries. In Cuba all the foreign exchange belongs to the public and is put to work implementing the country's development plans. Thus it is used to import productive goods that generate meaningful jobs such as building schools and homes and manufacturing basic home appliances and machinery. In the Dominican Republic a large part of the foreign exchange from sugar exports is treated as profit of private corporations such as Gulf and Western. Much of it is returned to the United States or wasted on projects such as G&W's tourist enclave that do not relate to the long-term development of the country. Such projects even represent an ongoing foreign exchange drain, for example, importing processed foods from home that tourists "need".

While we have concluded that export agriculture itself is not the enemy, we have come to see clearly that, minimally, *basic* food needs should be met locally. Basic food self-reliance—and by this we mean adequate local supplies to prevent famine if food imports abruptly jumped in price or were cut off—is the *sine qua non* of a people's security. Moreover, no country can bargain successfully in international trade so long as it is desperate to sell its products in order to import food to stave off famine.

Farmer plowing rice fields in the Phillipines. *Kay Chernush*

MYTH
SEVEN

The need to produce food conflicts with the goal of greater justice: redistributing control over resources would undercut production.

To many people, large agricultural entrepreneurs appear to have all the know-how and to have proven their efficiency by the simple fact of having gotten so big. Those with this view feel trapped: on the one hand, a food system increasingly controlled by a few cuts the majority out of land and jobs, making them hungry because they do not have access to the resources to secure food. On the other hand, if redistribution of control over resources were attempted, it is assumed that production would be undercut. People would then go hungry because there simply would not be enough food.

But this mental trap is an illusion. It assumes that an anti-democratic food system, where a few are in control, is actually the most productive when, in fact, such a food system inevitably under-uses and misuses food-producing resources.

First, concentration of control over productive resources leads to waste. In northeast Brazil, where the majority go hungry, large estates controlling most of the land actually cultivate only 15 percent.[75] The rest is used as pasture or left completely unused. Studies in Central America indicate that the largest landlords cultivate only 14 percent of their land.[76] Throughout the world, larger land-holders consistently produce less per acre than the small producers.[77]

Moreover, rural economists have concluded that when a few control the land, credit and marketing system in a village, as much as one-half to three-fourths of the value of agricultural production is siphoned out of the village.[78] It is not returned to the development of the area's agricultural resources. For those who own the land squander their profits on luxury consumer items or they "invest" in urban areas—tourist resorts, real estate, movie theaters, bars, taxi fleets, even foreign fast-food outlets. Likewise in the United States, sociologists have shown that when a few large operators control most of the land around a town, there are fewer parks, good roads, or stores and more unemployment. The wealth produced leaves town.[79]

Inequality in control over productive resources also leads to their underdevelopment. Inequality in control thwarts people's motivation to develop these resources. In Bangladesh[80] where about 90 percent of all the land is worked in whole or in part by tenants and day laborers,[81] a sharecropper may well feel: "Why should I apply more fertilizer or spend more time weeding? Wouldn't my work just benefit the landowner who gets most of whatever I grow?" Hired laborers, moreover, are concerned about their wages, not the landlord's yields. And since the landlord pays for their labor, he uses it sparingly.

The monopolization of control over resources also thwarts cooperation among people—cooperative work that is essential to development. In Bangladesh, cooperation in digging and maintaining ponds for irrigation and fish cultivation was common before

1793, the year the British instituted individual ownership of land. But today, when 10 percent of rural households have come to control 51 percent of the land and when almost half of the families have virtually no land, village-wide cooperative work is not possible. Many ponds, once a shared village asset, are now silted up and useless.

Inequality in control also leads to the destruction of productive resources. When the land is worked by tenants, sharecroppers and day laborers, the soil is often depleted, not protected. People who don't know if they will be working the same piece of land next year cannot be concerned about conserving it.

It is not just the tenant for whom conservation must take lowest priority. Farmer-owners, deeply in debt, are pitted for survival against all other farmers and dependent on monopoly-controlled high-priced inputs. They are forced to eke every bit of production out of the land each year no matter what that means in the long run. Notes one farm couple from Iowa:

> "We would like to plant more corn. It protects the soil. But we have two-thirds of our land in soybeans for the third year in a row. We know that soybeans let the soil blow away, but soybeans cost less to plant and bring a better price. If we planted more corn we'd be out of farming next year."[82]

In Haiti and Java, farmers forced off the fertile valley lands have to eke out a living on steep slopes, massively eroding the hills.

On the debt treadmill, farmers in the United States are also forced to plow up land that should be left as pasture. And they fail to let overused land lie fallow. According to the U.S. Soil Conservation Service, on much of the sloping land in Iowa a farmer is now losing two bushels of top soil for every one bushel of corn produced. At that rate all the topsoil in Iowa will be gone in less than a century.[83] Erosion is a major national problem.

An anti-democratic system, where a few are in control of the resources, also thwarts the efficient use of resources. An anthropologist wanted to understand why an Indian village she was studying required so many pumps to irrigate so little land. She was told that it is impossible to efficiently locate the pumps because the largest landowners insist on having the pumps serve their properties.[84]

Another important measure of the inefficient use of resources that results from their monopolization is simply *what* is grown. Those few landholders who control the majority of the farmland in the Third World grow what will bring the highest return on the highest paying market. Most local people are too poor to be in the market. So, in Central American and Caribbean countries, while as many as 80 percent of the children are undernourished, almost *half* the cultivated land, invariably the best, is used to grow just five of the commodities primarily produced for export: coffee, bananas, cocoa, sugar, and beef.[85] And in the Sahelian countries of Africa during the late 1960's and early 70's, elite-controlled economies in the Sahel continued to skew production toward exports even in the face of worsening drought and hunger. Exports of cotton, peanuts, vegetables, and meat to Western Europe actually increased.[86]

A final measure of the inefficiency of a food system where a few are in control is that it leads to the degradation of our food itself. Today we Americans are paying twice what we paid ten years ago for food—yet we get less. Half of all Americans now eat less than the recommended amounts of at least one nutrient—up from 15 percent 25 years ago.[87]

Food prices lead the inflation index. And 70 percent of the increase in our food costs over the last 25 years has gone to the processing-marketing sector where four or fewer corporations share monopoly control over many food lines including cereals, butter, cheese, sugar, vegetable oils, coffee and frozen foods.[88] With such tight control, these corporations can cut costs and raise profits. They increase what we spend on food, and their profit margins, by getting us to want more and more highly processed food. More preservatives, stabilizers, and other additives make possible further shipping and longer shelf lives—essential for corporations taking control of nationwide and even foreign foodmarketing.

Now to sum up. So many people have come to associate productivity with private control over resources and even with concentrated decison-making power. The attitude being—well, don't the big outfits have more know-how? Aren't they more efficient? Yet we have come to see that this system leads to monopoly control over resources in the interests of a few. Rather than being optimally productive, such a system leads inevitably to the *under-use* and *misuse* of resources.

So far we have touched on how counterproductive to democracy and to the needs of the majority is the system that so many have been taught to see as the most productive and even as the solution to hunger. But are there alternatives? When we at the Institute for Food and Development Policy study societies where people are eliminating hunger,[89] we find that their food economies do have certain features in common. While there are *no models*, we do find powerful lessons to be weighed from both the successes and the difficulties of people in other countries. Some of those key lessons we detail in our response to the next myth.

Cooperative fish hatchery in Vietnam. *Vietnam News Agency*

MYTH
EIGHT

Societies that have eliminated hunger have done so only by denying people's rights. There appears to be a trade-off between freedom and ending hunger.

This myth paralyzes well-meaning people perhaps more than any other. It raises critical questions that must be grappled with.

But a clear formulation of these questions is clouded by the multiple distortions contained in the myth.

First, it implies that societies that are *not* making structural changes to end hunger at least have more freedom. Even in terms of *theoretical* freedoms, this is often false. People in countries with widespread hunger and other forms of poverty, like the Philippines or Chile, do not have even the theoretical freedom to freely assemble or to vote.

Moreover, learning more about countries where many, often the majority, face hunger has forced us to confront the difference between theoretical freedoms and effective freedoms. In countries like India or Mexico, more and more people are losing control of their land. Still more find it hard to get any kind of job, even at slow starvation "wages". In such countries people have the theoretical freedom to organize and to vote. But do they effectively have the freedom? Given the violent reaction of the elite threatened by any mobilization of the poor, we doubt it. And while perhaps the most basic freedom is the freedom to achieve security for one's self and one's loved ones, in such countries—now the majority of the world's countries—life is increasingly insecure.

In other words, with absolutely no share in control over their country's productive assets, how much *effective* freedom do people have? This contradiction between theoretical freedom and effective freedom applies here in the United States as well.

Second, the myth seems to suggest that in eliminating hunger, countries have moved from a state of "more freedom" to less freedom. But when we study societies in which the majority are achieving greater food, job and old-age security—as in China or Cuba, for example—we find, of course, that people have not moved from a state of freedom to a state of repression in the process of achieving that security. No, the political and economic structures that preceded the present ones were among the most repressive in the world.

Studying these societies today, we find many problems—including the incredible difficulties resulting from hundreds of years of internal and external exploitation. Their problems are not only physical but human—how people can transform their consciousness of themselves in order to make true self-government possible. We also find the drive for greater self-government accompanied by some restrictions on people's individual choices. For many this might seem an untenable contradiction. But perhaps it is not. Perhaps it is rather an inevitable tension in societies attempting to create structures to meet the needs of all.

In such an attempt the legal definition of what is socially harmful might have to be enlarged. In our system we allow speculation in land and food that insures that some persons go hungry while others profiteer and many over-consume. In a system attempting deliberately to plan for the needs of all, hoarding and speculation are not accepted. (Most important, of course, most people seem not so motivated to hoard and speculate when their basic needs for a job and food are assured.) Moreover, individual choices may sometimes have to be adjusted in order to fulfill the community's needs. At least during the primary period of overcoming underdevelopment some may not be able to choose whatever job or location they prefer. (We must keep in mind of course that few even in supposedly free market societies have such absolute freedom.) Clearly, every society places limits upon the individual's choices. The real issues then are these: How can those restrictions be made fairly? Are the restrictions imposed by an elite for their benefit or imposed by the community for the good of all? Is the goal to achieve a society in which the individual's legitimate self-interest and the community's needs are more and more complementary?

Freedom for critical expression is also of pivotal concern. In countries that choose to break with the private control over productive assets this issue is made considerably more problematic by the denunciation, aggressive posturing, and even subversive intervention of foreign powers like the United States. Such external hostility creates the worst possible environment for the fostering of internal critical expression (and individual variety). Americans should know this all too well from the years following Pearl Harbor. Any individual or grouping of individuals differing with the commonly held view runs the risk of being labeled a collaborator of the foreign enemy. The challenge for a society in the difficult period of restructuring is both to recognize the vulnerability caused by a lack of unity, and yet to develop effective means for constructive critical thinking. Critical thinking must be encouraged, thinking that can speak out and be heard *even* when at first few acknowledge the very existence of an issue, as with nuclear power or sexism.

Thus, instead of the simplistic notion that "freedom" must be sacrificed to eliminate hunger, we find tremendous complexity. But we also find grounds for hope. While no people on earth has achieved a model society which ideally melds individual and community needs, we do have much to learn from people engaged in the *process* of attempting that goal.

One lesson to be learned is that when people are actively involved in deciding how resources are to be used, not only will they benefit but also production is likely to increase. Consider the Chinese experience.[90] Through a series of innovations, the Chinese people have moved to ownership and control of the land directly by those who work the fields. Work is determined by the production team—a village unit of 30 or 40 families. The result is a significant reduction in rural inequality: the gap between the richest and poorest in the rural population in China is only one-fourth as great as in most Asian countries. Food production has climbed consistently and, as we have already noted, there has been no famine since at least the early 1960's. In order further to increase agricultural production in the 1980's, the production team is taking on even greater authority over production. Similarly, according to a recent study of Cuban agriculture, the greater production successes of the 1970's are significantly related to greater popular participation in decision-making and responsibility.[91]

A second lesson is the need for community-based but society-wide planning. Many have been taught to associate planning with a totalitarian form of top-down government. Such a simplistic association ignores two basic facts. First, in a supposedly non-planned, privately controlled economy, planning, of course, does go on. Only the planning is done primarily by the few who control the productive assets and for their own benefit. Second, planning need not be a solely top-down affair. Indeed, experience shows that top-down planning cannot be effective.

Effective social planning can only result from the decentralization of authority that allows each region to work out appropriate solutions. Effective planning is not simply establishing quotas, targets and tasks; it is the organization of a sensitive and flexible structure of communication between government bodies and communities.

The Chinese call this "from the people/to the people" social planning, in which the nutritional needs of all the people are translated into a national agricultural plan. A Canadian report on agriculture and nutrition in Cuba describes how local farmers participate in this translation: "Meetings take place with all the farm workers and small farmers at the local level to discuss the plan and the production quotas allocated to their area. Suggestions for revisions or changes are made. This feedback process is very important because it is the local farmers who know best what crops will grow in their area."[92]

Such planning substitutes conscious intervention and co-operation for the free market. Social planning does not preclude the market altogether; the difference is that in a society whose conscious goal is to meet the needs of all the people, social planning can "utilize the market instead of being governed by it," observes United Nations development economist J. B. W. Kuitenbrouwer.[93]

There is yet a third lesson that would be overlooked if we simply "write off" all non-capitalist development. That lesson is this: agriculture can no longer be viewed as a mine from which to extract wealth to serve other sectors. As we pointed out in Myth Four, this lesson has not been learned in the United States. Here deterioration of the livelihoods and culture of rural people as well as of rural resources goes hand in hand with massive agricultural production for export.

By contrast the Chinese grasped that a healthy rural economy is the basis of any society. The Chinese planners, for example, from the 1950's onward, favored agriculture. They reduced the costs of farmers' supplies. Farmers' taxes were kept small. And they did not go up as production went up. Thus, farm producers increasingly benefitted from their labor. They could use the profits from their production to increase consumption and reinvest in tools, education, and medical care.

The fourth and perhaps most important lesson is that the first three lessons represent a *process* and not simply goals that are achieved once and for all. And within this process are profound tensions — the tensions between the individual's wishes and the community needs; the tension between democratic, participatory decision-making and the need for leadership based on specialized skills, knowledge and experience; the tension between a focus on agriculture and the need to build up industry as necessary to increase agricultural productivity.

These are just a few of what we have come to believe are *necessary* tensions in creating a social, economic, and political system designed to maximize both individual fulfillment and community progress. The trouble with a "freedom versus food trade-off" as posited in Myth Eight is that by over-simplifying and distorting it frightens people, preventing them from being able to learn from the valuable experience of their counterparts in other countries.

South Korean company executive talks with AID advisor in front of flour bags purchased with Cooley Loans. *U.S. Agency for International Development*

MYTH
NINE

To help the hungry we should improve and increase our foreign aid programs.

Many concerned Americans believe that where elite-controlled structures generate hunger we should intervene to "improve the lot of the poor." They focus on improving and increasing official U. S. foreign assistance.

They call for "new directions-style aid"—focus on the small farmer, basic needs, support for land reform, appropriate technology, and popular participation. But they presume at least two things: first, that official development assistance is the principal way the U.S. government intervenes in the struggle for food security in countries around the world; and second, that U.S.-funded aid agencies actually are doing, or even could do, what they say they are doing—helping the poor and hungry.

Focusing on official development assistance and its relationship to the hungry threatens to divert attention of concerned Americans from the many other and often more telling ways their government affects the poor majority in other countries. For U.S. government development aid is the proverbial tip of the iceberg. There are at least 15 other overt channels (not to mention covert ones like the CIA) through which the U.S. government supports the governments and economic elites of its choosing. Here we mention only a few:

U.S. military sales and assistance programs to Third World countries are projected for 1979 at over $9 billion—well in excess of four times the total budget of A.I.D. (the official U.S. development assistance agency).[94] Military assistance and sales programs shore up regimes that both block democratic control over food-producing resources and suppress the right to work to change structures that generate hunger. Can we conceivably, through "development assistance" to a foreign government, help the poor at the same time as we train and arm the police and military who terrorize, beat, shoot, torture and imprison the poor and their allies?

Despite explicit congressional prohibition against military assistance and sales to "gross violators of internationally recognized human rights," military assistance and arms sales in 1978 continued to *at least* nine dictatorships widely denounced for their violation of human rights: Nicaragua, Indonesia, the Philippines, Thailand, Bangladesh, South Korea, Zaire, Paraguay, and Haiti. Are not these military aid recipients more threatened by their own poor majority than by some external threat? For in each of these countries we find active, widespread popular resistance; in some, clearly U.S. military aid has made the crucial difference for oppressive elites to be able so far to hold the line. President Carter, in 1979, concluded a $1.5 billion economic and military aid package to the Marcos dictatorship in the Philippines, where arms and training go to combat growing resistance to a regime whose policies have led to grain consumption per person falling to the lowest in all of Asia.[95]

The Treasury Department's Export-Import Bank and the Commodity Credit Corporation offer financing and loan guarantees on favorable terms to foreign purchasers of U.S. products. Such support massively outstrips official foreign aid. In a typical year, about double the U.S. government support reaches Third World countries through the Export-Import Bank alone than through the entire budget of AID (excluding the Security Supporting Assistance.)[96] When in 1976 human rights protests forced the Chilean junta to reject U.S. development aid, financing through the Export-Import Bank and the Commodity Credit Corporation overwhelmingly made up for the lost aid.[97]

The International Monetary Fund (IMF) is a fund from which 130 member nations can borrow foreign currency to help meet short-term balance of payments deficits.[98] Of the many financial institutions influencing the economies — and therefore the people — of the underdeveloped countries, perhaps it is the most powerful yet the least in public view. The United States holds the largest voting block and veto power.

When a country's debt burden and trade deficits mount and it cannot get loans from private international banks, it must turn to the IMF. The IMF is not only a lender of last resort but an international financial auditor whose approval is essential to get bank and governmental loans. But before giving approval, the IMF stipulates a number of domestic economic measures that must be carried out. Governments and private banks hold off lending to a country until it has secured the IMF's stamp of approval.

To get this approval, a country is usually obliged to: devalue its currency so as to boost exports and limit imports, cut back public spending programs, introduce wage controls, lift price controls on even the most essential food items, raise interest rates, and remove barriers to foreign investment and free trade. Free trade means that luxury items are still allowed to enter even when scarce foreign exchange should be going for more needed basic items. These measures benefit foreign agribusiness and other corporations extracting cheap labor and resources; the burden falls mainly on all the working people and squarely on the poor.

But even putting to one side for a moment the reality that official development aid is only the tip of the iceberg, what do we find when we examine U.S. aid programs in themselves?

First, where does the money go? U.S. aid is highly concentrated on only a small number of countries. In 1979 over 50 percent of U.S. development assistance went to only ten countries;* only four of these are considered "low income."[99] As much U.S. development assistance goes to Egypt, Israel and Jordan as to all the other countries of Asia, Africa and Latin America. Countries such as South Korea and the Philippines rank among these top ten because of their strategic military location and "open door" policies for multinational corporations.

Clearly, recipient governments are chosen more on the basis of

---

* Egypt, Israel, India, Indonesia, Bangladesh, Pakistan, Syria, Philippines, Jordan, South Korea.

their supposed importance to the United States than on their poverty or genuine commitment to development. In fact U.S. policy has been to cut off aid when genuine agrarian reforms are underway, for example, in Chile and in Thailand. Whereas when governments, often through the introduction of martial law dictatorships, actively undermine the well-being of the majority and abolish civil liberties in order to deal with those who protest, U.S. aid seems to get vastly stepped up. Aid to Thailand and the Philippines increased severalfold after martial law dictatorships brutally attacked peasant groups and all others organizing for reforms.

And what about the allocation priorities of the World Bank—the world's largest lender for "development" and where the U.S. government has the largest voting share (23 percent). Once again, looking at the list of World Bank loan recipients, we find a heavy bias in favor of a few countries where the poor majority are cut out ever more from sharing in control of the productive resources: Brazil, Indonesia, Mexico, India, the Philippines, Egypt, Colombia and South Korea received well over half of total Bank lending in 1978.[100] Only two of the top ten Bank loan recipients are deemed "low income" by the Bank's own standards: India and Indonesia. Yet in India increasing inequalities translate into hunger and poverty for millions while surplus grains and several billion dollars worth of foreign exchange reserves accumulate.[101] In Indonesia an elite military regime has been squandering the country's oil wealth while, as the *Wall Street Journal* notes, "the government won't even allow the landless [85% of the rural families] to organize pressure groups."[102] Martial law dictatorships are prevalent among the top recipients: South Korea, the Philippines and Brazil. And, consistent with U.S. Priorities in the Middle East, the Bank is channeling sizeable credits to Egypt.

But forget for a minute the above points. Let us assume that U.S. aid programs truly go to the countries most in need. What is the impact of the programs themselves? What do our aid dollars do?

It is not fashionable of late to defend "trickle down" theory—the notion that investments in physical infrastructures will help the economy and therefore eventually help the poor. But even a cursory survey of AID, as well as World Bank or regional bank programs, reveals that "trickle down" still prevails. In many countries the major outlays of AID and of the World Bank (approximately two thirds of total lending in the Bank's case) continue to be for infrastructure projects—especially highways, dams, electrification—that at best benefit those who already control a country's productive assets and, as we discussed in response to Myth Three, further concentrate that control and thereby erode the situation of the poor. In northeast Brazil the World Bank is helping finance a $400 million hydroelectric and irrigation scheme. A 200-mile long stretch along the Sao Francisco will be flooded evicting 70,000 small farm families, few of whom are being provided with any decent alternatives. The electricity will go to the coastal cities. The irrigated farms created will be elite-owned, mechanized and geared towards producing for export.[103]

Not surprisingly, defining development in terms of such projects boosts the sales of what multinational corporations have to sell. In the spirit of "appropriate terminology," AID often lists such projects under the heading "Food and Nutrition". For instance, here are but a few of such outlays cloaked under "Food and Nutrition" in the *Fiscal 1979 Presentation to Congress:* "$100 Million Rural Roads Phase II in Pakistan"; $36 Million Rural Electrification in Indonesia; $10.3 Million "Fund for Local Government in the Philippines." The chief of the AID agricultural mission in Indonesia had to agree with us that the principal beneficiaries of a $125 million AID electrification project will be the better-off farmers who would use the electricity to mill rice mechanically. Traditional rice-hulling jobs for the poor, especially women, will be eliminated.

If "trickle down" is out, "small farmer" is in. Helping the small farmer has come to be equated by many with progressive change. Unfortunately, however, it is not that simple. First, even *if* the small peasant producers were to become the focus of foreign assistance, there would still be no effective strategy for the real rural dispossessed—the landless and near-landless (day laborers, insecure tenants, sharecroppers, and squatters) who make up 30 to 85 percent of the rural labor force.[104] Indeed, some programs that aim at helping small farmers would, if successful, actually *worsen* the situation of this huge stratum of the rural poor.[105] With increased income, small farmers tend to buy up additional land. And supplying even the most small-scale technology to small landholders could eliminate jobs desperately needed by the landless who must sell their labor—and that of their children—in order to survive.

But the reality is that even AID programs earmarked for the small farmers rarely reach them. For, in part, this depends on how AID agencies define "small." In Panama, AID—financed credit programs were made available to any farm of 50 acres or less.[106] Now, such a standard might identify small farmers in the United States, but not in Panama. There, 50 percent of those rural people who have any land have less than ten acres—and most, a lot less. In Guatemala a World Bank credit scheme for "small farmers" in fact allocates one-half of the credit to the biggest three percent of all landowners.[107] The other half is "for those with less than 112 acres"— as if this were the appropriate cut-off line to identify small farmers. In fact, 87 percent of Guatemalan farmers have less than 17 acres. Another example is Nicaragua. There the government pushed an

AID-funded credit program limit up to $590 per farmer.[108] $590 is five times the annual income of 70 percent of the rural people in Nicaragua. What is to prevent such a loan program from being monopolized by the better-off?

The focus of such AID and World Bank credit programs is to increase smallholder productivity through the greater use of agricultural inputs. But smallholders who are poor and hungry are so primarily not because of lack of inputs but lack of economic and political bargaining power. With no increase in that power, will their increased output benefit them? More likely, credit programs focusing only on production will lead to plummeting prices of what the poor produce and thus to more indebtedness. The main beneficiaries? The merchants, moneylenders, and other exploiters in the rural hierarchy who will continue to siphon off the lion's share. These realizations lead us to conclude that there is an enormous difference between increasing the productivity of the poor (as AID and the World Bank so righteously claim to be doing) and being interested in promoting the livelihood and well-being of the poor.

Nor is it likely that cooperative organizations set up to channel credits and farm inputs to "small farmers" will function equitably in a social setting of significant inequalities. We have to conclude from first-hand investigations as well as those of others around the world that supposed cooperatives wind up in the control of the better-off landowners in the area and usually to the detriment of small marginal farmers and the landless. As one Swedish government evaluation of aid-funded village cooperative programs in Bangladesh concluded, "To try to keep the big landowners outside the cooperatives . . . . is nothing but wishful thinking."[109]

Many poor rural people are aware that their only hope is to organize themselves to pressure for changes—not hand-out programs from aid agencies. In the Guatemalan highlands last year, for instance, organized farmers refused to accept AID money.[110]

The humanitarian value of chronic food aid shipments has also been called into question by many. Conventional wisdom has shifted: now even U.S. government agencies (such as the General Accounting Office[111]) agree that food aid rarely reaches the hungry or even gets out of a country's urban areas. Instead it becomes a principal form of budgetary support for the recipient governments as well as a depressant on prices for locally produced agricultural products. Local producers are further impoverished and discouraged from producing.

But food aid, too, has been dressed up: development experts are now pushing "food-for-work" programs. At best food-for-work projects provide some rural workers with a meager income for a specific period. They do nothing, however, to change the ownership and power structures that produce unemployment in the first place. Indeed such projects in the long term enhance the power of the already better-off landholders who, for instance, can use the new road to get their produce out to market. Food-for-work projects can function to take the edge off a potentially explosive rural situation by providing a few jobs during the slack agricultural season. A recent study by the F.A.O. stressed that food-for-work programs "lend themselves to misappropriation of grain, misuse of funds, false reporting of works, creation of a new class of profiteers, poor quality construction, etc."[112]

Our Institute has received in 1978 several communications, independent of each other, from American missionaries in rural Haiti who decry food-for-work programs using U.S. food aid. One wrote:

> In the village where we are living, for example, one family controls all the community and government offices including judge, mayor, community council, president, etc. Besides owning vast tracts of land, "the family" speculates in coffee and controls all the illegal tree-cutting in the area. When CARE entered the village with a Food for Work soil conservation project (using U.S. food aid), it came as no surprise that "the family" was the local administrator of the project and chose who would work in the project. "The family," through the auspices of the community council president, is also responsible for seeing to the actual food distribution. To the CARE people this project is a good grassroots effort, but in reality it is not helping those peasants in the area who really need it. CARE, for example, believes that the workers are mostly landless peasants. We have surveyed nearly all of the workers on the project and have yet to find any landless peasants. The workers must work 3 days a week on the project, 1 day on the road for the community council and 1 day in the garden of one of the community leaders (i.e., "the family"). Thus the projects take the farmers away from their own plots for 5 days of the week.

Finally, even if our government wanted to shift its entire aid program to put itself on the side of the hungry throughout the world, could it do so? We have had to conclude that no governmental development assistance program can address the social and economic causes of hunger because in doing so it would threaten the very elites with whom overall U.S. policy must maintain relations. Clearly U.S. aid policy will not go against the elites abroad who serve U.S. military and corporate interests; it *must* side with the elites who are resisting challenges to an economic system similar to that of the United States.

Young Thai farmer. *World Bank photo by M. Bolotsky.*

MYTH
TEN

Peasants are so underfed, so ignorant of the real forces oppressing them and conditioned into a state of passivity that they are beyond the point of being able to mobilize themselves.

Bombarded with pictures showing the poor as weak and hungry, we should not lose sight of the obvious fact that they often must exert themselves tremendously just to stay alive—traveling long distances and working 10 to 14 hours a day. In at least that sense, the poor are hardly passive. They represent great potential energy that, once released, could be applied to their own development.

Moreover, many living and working with the poor in underdeveloped countries often have been astonished at how well they comprehend the forces oppressing them. In a report for the U. N. Asian Development Institute, the four Asian authors with much experience in organizing with the rural poor concluded that the poor "have an understanding of the working of the economic system and can describe in detail the processes (wage exploitation, money lending, bribery and price discrimination) through which exploitation takes place."[113]

Those with direct experience working with poor peasants also counter the notion that it is mainly superstitious religious beliefs that keep the poor down. Lasse and Lisa Berg, writing of their experiences in India in their book *Face to Face*, observe that, while reasoning based in religious beliefs might characterize India's middle class, the poor almost never cite religion to explain their daily actions. "If asked why they do not revolt," note the Bergs, "they do not answer that they want to be reborn to a better position; they answer that they are afraid of the landowner or the government or the police."[114]

But stressing both the powerful structure of control over the lives of the poor and their understandable fear can cause us to ignore the fact that *in every country in the world where people are hungry there is a struggle going on right now over who controls food-producing resources*—in Mexico, the Philippines, South Africa, Brazil, Chad, the United States, El Salvador, Bangladesh, Thailand and we could go on and on. Among those standing up to resist are the very people who have been perceived by so many as "too oppressed ever to change." For us the question is: on whose side *in fact* are we?

Moreover, so many who would question what peasants can do seem unaware that there are countries such as Vietnam, Mozambique, Guinea Bissau and Angola where, after decades of intense struggle, mainly by peasant-based organizations, independence has recently been won. Now these people are turning their energies into eradicating hunger and building the basis of genuine food security. Neither must one forget that since only the early 1950's, over 40 percent of the population of the underdeveloped world have freed themselves from the fear of famine through their own efforts.

Because of the selective way news is transmitted to us, we in countries like the United States are often unaware of the courageous struggles of millions of people everywhere to gain control over food-producing resources rightfully theirs.

Events often come to us filtered through a lens that causes us to identify not with people like us, but with the governing elites in underdeveloped countries. We once read, for example, a news account of the depressed economy of Senegal, ruined by a fall-off in production of the main export crop, peanuts. Simply presented this way, our natural response was to ask: What can be done to spur the lagging production of this crop? How can we help to get the economy rolling again? We thus were made to identify with the export economy of Senegal, not with the people.

The real story was that many Senegalese peasants had purposefully spurned cash-cropping in order to grow food for themselves, particularly millet and sorghum. This shift was interpreted by some as the reaction of tradition-bound peasants. On the contrary, this example of peasant resistance can be seen as a positive break away from tradition, if being traditional means doing what the political and social hierarchy has always demanded. These lessons are seldom, if ever, drawn for us; such is the power of selective news that reinforces the notion of the passivity of the world's disenfranchised.

To counter the myth of the passive poor we must find ongoing sources of news that go behind the selective, filtered information offered us by most of the media. At the end of this booklet we therefore include a list of some of the publications and organizations that provide news and analysis of the struggles of ordinary people in countries around the world for their food rights. We find these sources invaluable in uprooting the myth of the passive poor and the companion myth, that of our own powerlessness.

What Can We Do?

First, we must begin with the self-evident but often forgotten truth that people can and will feed themselves. Everywhere that they are not doing so, we find powerful obstacles in the way of people taking control of food-producing resources and feeding themselves. We should not see our role as intervening in other countries and "setting things right." Rather we must ask ourselves what key obstacles to people taking charge of their lives are right now being built with our taxes, in our name and by corporations based in our economies. And how can we join the people already working to overthrow those obstacles?

Our tasks are very clear:

Work to halt U.S. military and counter-insurgency assistance to underdeveloped countries; it is used against those working for the changes necessary for abolishing hunger.

Work to end all support for agribusiness penetration into food economies abroad from governments and multilateral lending agencies and through tax incentives and other federal programs (such as the Overseas Private Investment Corporation).

Work to end foreign assistance to governments working against the food security of their people. We can start by demonstrating to those who now seek a solution to hunger through official foreign assistance how their energies are *misfocused*. In exposing how U.S. foreign assistance shores up repressive regimes, we are teaching a powerful lesson about the present nature of our own government.

Work to limit U.S. foreign assistance only to those countries where a genuine redistribution of power over productive assets is underway. Such aid should be in the form of grants, untied to purchases in the United States. Only in this way will aid not reinforce patterns of debt dependency.

Work to build a democratically controlled and food self-reliant economy in America. Urge democratization of access to land, credit and farm technology. Work to end absentee ownership of our country's food resources.

Support the unionization of farm workers, as well as worker-managed production units, i.e., family farms and cooperatives, and worker-managed distribution systems to replace the system of concentrated multinational corporate control over our food resources.

Promote investigative research. The mobilization of public support for the necessary changes will require much new and concrete documentation. You and your group might choose to concentrate on the area where you live.

Educate. Show the connections between the way the U.S. government and agribusiness oligopolies work against the hungry abroad and the way they work against the food interests of the vast majority of people in our own country.

Counter despair. Communicate that countries thought to be hopelessly poor and passive have freed themselves from hunger. Counter despair, but not by painting an idealized picture of alternatives. Underestimating the problems can only end up increasing despair. Communicate that in committing ourselves to this terribly difficult process we do not have to start the train moving: In every country brave, ordinary people are already fighting for their food rights.

To commit ourselves to any of the above "tasks" is to understand that to be part of structural change that can alleviate the profound deprivation and insecurity of so many of the world's people—including our own—we have to be in for the "long haul." Moreover, we find that our commitment to end world hunger will affect every aspect of our lives, once we decide to let it. We must be open to asking: How does each of our life decisions reinforce the present structure of economic control that generates hunger? How can we begin now to take responsibility for creating an economic system that can eliminate hunger?

While we, of course, do not claim to have all of the answers to these fundamental questions, we hope you will want to join with us in a search for their answers. Other publications of our Institute*, as well as other resources listed in the following pages, we hope will serve as useful guides to appropriate action for you.

The first step for each of us, however, is to break through the powerful myths that have kept us divided and fearful and to begin to realize that we can be part of a worldwide movement, allying ourselves with hungry people everywhere.

---

*See the announcements at the end of this booklet.

Ten
Food First
Fundamentals

We can now counter the ten myths presented here with ten positive fundamentals that could ground a coherent and vital movement:

1. Every country in the world has the resources necessary for its people to free themselves from hunger.

2. To balance a country's population and resources, it is urgent to address now the root cause of both hunger and high birth rates: the insecurity and poverty of the majority that results from the control over basic national resources by a few.

3. Hunger is only made worse when approached as a technical problem. Hunger can only be overcome by the majority first transforming the social structures so that they directly participate in building a democratic economic system.

4. Safeguarding the world's agricultural environment and people freeing themselves from hunger are complementary goals.

5. The hungry are our allies, not our enemies nor a perpetual burden. Our food security is not threatened by hungry people but by a system that concentrates economic power into the hands of elites who profit by the generation of scarcity and the internationalization of food control.

6. Export agriculture is not the enemy. But in a society where only a few control the productive resources, export-oriented agriculture strengthens the grip of those elites. To insure food security, agriculture must become, first and foremost, a way for people to produce their food and livelihood and secondarily a possible source of foreign exchange.

7. Justice and production are complementary goals. The most wasteful and inefficient food system is one controlled by a few in the interests of a few.

8. Hunger cannot be eliminated by denying people's freedom but by encouraging participation in decision-making. In order to achieve freedom from the fear of hunger for everyone, however, it may be necessary to limit the choices of some. This ongoing tension between the right of everyone for basic security and the right of the individual for freedom of choice is one that exists within every society.

9. The appropriate response of Americans to hunger abroad is not more or even improved government foreign "aid". We must work instead to help remove the obstacles in the way of people's efforts for self-determination, especially those obstacles being built by U.S. economic and military interventions abroad and by the penetration of U.S.-based corporations.

10. Our role is not to go in and "set things right," for wherever people are hungry there are already many ordinary, brave men and women working to democratize the control over food-producing resources.

Notes

1. Calculated from FAO Production Yearbooks. Figures for recent years indicate global grain production is approximately 2.2 pounds per person per day.

2. "India: Plenty of Cash, Food—Still In Need," *Los Angeles Times,* March 26, 1978, p. 9.

3. Letter from Dr. Marcel Ganzin, Director, Food Policy and Nutrition Division, FAO, Rome, dated December 18, 1975.

4. Alan Riding, "Malnutrition Taking Bigger Toll Among Mexican Children," *The New York Times,* March 6, 1978, page 2.

5. Calculated from FAO *Production Yearbook,* 1977.

6. Institute of Nutrition and Food Science, *Nutrition Survey of Rural Bangladesh,* University of Dacca, Bangladesh 1977.

7. Interview by Michael Scott of Oxfam-America, Boston.

8. Dr. Benedict Stavis, Cornell University, personal communication, December, 1976.

9. Calculated from Food and Agriculture Organization, *Production Yearbook,* Vol. 28-1, 1974.

10. Acreage comparison from Production Yearbook, Vol. 28-1, 1974, FAO and nutritional data from Dr. Georg Borgstrom, personal communication, April, 1977.

11. Ibid, *Production Yearbook.*

12. Samir Amin, "L'Afrique sous peuplee," *Development et Civilisation,* nos. 47-48, March-June, 1972: 60-61.

13. Calculated from FAO *Production Yearbook,* 1974.

14. *The World Food Problem: A Report of the President's Science Advisory Committee,* Washington, DC: Government Printing Office, 1967, Tables 7-9, p. 434; see also Leroy L. Blakeslee, Earl O. Heady, and Charles F. Framingham, "World Food Production, Demand and Trade," Iowa State University, 1973.

15. Calculated from FAO *Production Yearbooks.*

16. Betsy Hartmann and James Boyce, *Needless Hunger: Voices From a*

Bangladesh Village, San Francisco: Institute for Food and Development Policy, 1979.

17. *World Hunger, Health and Refugee Problems, Summary of a Special Study Mission to Asia and the Middle East,* Washington DC: U.S. Government Printing Office, 1976, p. 99.

18. Robert d' A. Shaw, *Jobs and Agricultural Development,* Washington DC: Overseas Development Council, 1970, Table 2, p. 10.

19. World Bank, *The Assault on World Poverty,* Baltimore: Johns Hopkins University Press, 1975, pp. 242-243.

20. Calculated from FAO Production Yearbooks.

21. Food and Agriculture Organization, *Report on 1960 Census of World Agriculture,* Rome, Italy; and Milton J. Esman, *Landlessness and Near Landlessness in Developing Countries,* Ithaca, New York: Center for International Studies, Cornell University, 1978.

22. World Bank, *The Assault on World Poverty,* Washington, D.C., 1975, p. 105.

23. United Nations Research Institute for Social Development, Multi-Volume Study of *The Social and Economic Implications of the Large-Scale Introduction of New Varieties of Food Grains,* Geneva, Switzerland; also, Keith Griffin and A.R. Khan, *Landlessness and Poverty in Rural Asia,* prepared for the International Labor Organization, Geneva, 1976.

24. Cynthia Hewitt de Alcántara, *The Social and Economic Implications of the Large-Scale Introduction of New Varieties of Food Grains, Country Report—Mexico,* Geneva: UNDP/UNRISD, 1974, p. 30 (This manuscript became published; document cited as 25.); "Mexico: Roosting Chickens," *Latin America* (Nov. 28, 1975), p. 375.

25. Cynthia Hewitt de Alcántara, *Modernizing Mexican Agriculture,* Geneva: United Nations Research Institute for Social Development, 1976, p. 318.

26. *New York Times,* March 3, 1976, p. 2.

27. Gail Omvedt, journalist living in Poona, India, forthcoming manuscript.

28. Keith Griffin and Azizur Rahman Khan, eds., *Poverty and Landlessness in Rural Asia,* A Study by the World Employment Programme, Geneva: ILO, 1976, manuscript.

29. Global II Project on the Social and Economic Implications of the Large-Scale Introduction of New Varieties of Food Grains, United Nations Research Institute for Social Development, Geneva.

30. Michael Perelman, *Farming for Profit in a Hungry World*, Montclair, N.J.: Allanheld, Osmun, 1977, p. 88.

31. U. S. Department of Agriculture, *Farm Income Statistics*, Statistical Bulletin no. 547, July 1975; and U. S. Department of Agriculture, *Agriculture Statistics 1972*.

32. Emergency Land Fund, Atlanta, Georgia.

33. U. S. General Accounting Office, *Changing Character and Structure of American Agriculture: An Overview*, Washington D. C. , September 26, 1978, p. 104.

34. Robert C. Fellmeth, *Politics of Land*, Ralph Nader's Study Group Report on Land Use in California, New York: Grossman, 1973, p. 12, based on "A Statistical Profile of California Corporate Farmers," Agricultural Extension Service of the University of California and the Economic Research Service of USDA, 1969.

35. U. S. Department of Agriculture, *Our Land and Water Resources*, USDA/ERS Misc. Publication No. 1290, 1974, p. 32.

36. John E. Lee, Jr., "Agricultural Finance, Situation and Issues," Paper presented at the 1978 Food and Agricultural Outlook Conference, USDA, Washington, D.C., November 1977 (mimeo).

37. U. S. General Accounting Office, *Changing Character and Structure of American Agriculture: An Overview*, Washington D.C., September 26, 1978, p. 7.

38. Council on Wage and Price Stability, Executive Office of the President, *Report on Prices for Agricultural Machinery and Equipment*, Washington D.C., 1976.

39. Jim Hightower, *Eat Your Heart Out*, New York: Random House, 1976, p. 172.

40. Joseph Hanlon, "India Back to the Village: Does A. T. Walk on Plastic Sandals?" *New Scientist*, May 26, 1977, p. 467 ff.

41. David Pimentel, et al, *"Pesticides, Insects in Foods, and Cosmetic Standards*, Bio Science, vol. 27, no. 3 March, 1977, p. 180.

42. *Ibid.*

43. *Ibid.*

44. *The AgBiz Tiller*, San Francisco Study Center, PO Box 5646, San Francisco, CA 94101, No. 3 (November 1976), p. 1.

45. David Pimentel, "Realities of a Pesticide Ban," *Environment*, 15 March 1973.

46. J. P. Hrabovszky, Senior Policy and Planning Coordinator, Agriculture Department, FAO, Rome, letter dated March 18, 1976, quoting Dr. W. R. Furtick, Chief, Plant Protection Service.

47. Personal communication of L. Moore and T. F. Watson with Dr. Robert van den Bosch, Division of Biological Control, University of California, Berkeley, cited by Dr. van den Bosch in "The Politics of Pesticides," speech, 1973.

48. Erich H. Jacoby, *The Green Revolution in China*, Geneva: UNRISD, December 18, 1973, pp 11-12.

49. Based on interview with officer of Inter-American Development Bank.

50. *The Economic Development of Colombia*, Baltimore: Johns Hopkins University Press, 1950, pp. 63 and 360, cited in Michael Hudson, *Super Imperialism*, New York: Holt, Rinehart and Winston, 1972, pp. 103-104.

51. Jose S. Da Veiga, "Quand les multinationales font du ranching," *Le Monde Diplomatique*, September 1975, p. 12.

52. Based on Kenneth E. Grant, "Erosion in 1973-1974: The Record and the Challenge," *Journal of Soil and Water Conservation*, 30:1, Jan-Feb 1974, cited in Michael Perelman, *Farming for Profit in a Hungry World*, Montclair: Allanheld, Osmun, 1977.

53. David Pimentel, et al, "Land Degradation: Effects on Food and Energy Resources," *Science*, vol. 194, October 8, 1976, p. 152.

54. William Brune, State Conservationist, Soil Conservation Service, Des Moines, Iowa, Testimony before Senate Committee on Agriculture and Forestry, July 6, 1976; see also Seth King, "Iowa Rain and Wind Deplete Farmlands," *New York Times*, December 5, 1976, p. 61.

55. "Wheels of Fortune: A Report on the Impact of Center Pivot Irrigation on the Ownership of Land in Nebraska," Center for Rural Affairs, PO Box 405, Walthill, Nebraska, 68067. See also "No One Knows the Value of Water Until the Well Runs Dry," *New Land Review* (Spring 1976), p. 3, also published by the Center for Rural Affairs.

56. National Commission on Food Marketing, *The Structure of Food Manufacturing*. A report by the staff of the Federal Trade Commission (Technical Study No. 8), June 1966, p. 19.

57. Linda Grant Martin, "How Beatrice Foods Sneaked up on $5 billion," *Fortune*, April 1976, cited in Susan George *Feeding the Few*, Washington D. C. : Transnational Institute, 1979.

58. The following sources confirm this rough estimation: John M. Connor and Losy L. Mather, Directory of 200 Largest U. S. Food and Tobacco Processing Firms, 1975, Economics Statistics and Cooperatives Service, USDA, and North Central Regional Project NC-117, July, 1978 and Russell C. Parker and John M. Connor, "Estimates of Consumer Loss Due to Monopoly in the U. S. Food Manufacturing Industries," Food Systems Research Group of North Central Research Project NC-117, University of Wisconsin, Madison, Wisconsin, 1978.

59. Ibid., Parker and Connor.

60. Joint Economic Committee, U. S. Congress, The Profit and Price Performance of Leading Food Chains, 1970-74, Washington, D. C. : U. S. Government Printing Office, May 6, 1977.

61. 1972-1973 Consumer Expenditure Survey, Bureau of Labor Statistics, U. S. Department of Labor.

62. Dan Morgan, Merchants of Grain: The Power and Profits of the Five Great Companies at the Center of the World Food Supply, New York; Viking, 1979.

63. Transnational Institute, Unilever's World, Nottingham, England: Russell Press Ltd. Counter-Information Service Anti-Report No. 11, C1S No. 52 Shaftesbury Ave, London W1 England.

64. Frederick Clairmonte, "Bananas" in Cheryl Payer, ed., Commodity Trade in the Third World, New York: Wiley, 1975.

65. Ray Goldberg, Agribusiness Management in Developing Countries—Latin America, Cambridge, Mass: Ballinger, 1974, p. 70.

66. U.S. Department of Agriculture, Economic Research Service, Tom Warden and Richard Kennedy, December, 1977.

67. U.S. Department of Agriculture, U.S. Foreign Agricultural Trade Statistical Report Calendar Year 1977, Economics, Statistics and Cooperative Service, USDA, Washington, D.C., 1978.

68. Bangkok Post, January 26, 1978, p. 1. Cassava has now (1979) become the number one export, most of it going to Western Europe to feed cattle.

69. Departamento de Economia Agraria, Pontificia Universidad Catolica de Chile, Panorama Economico de la Agricultura, November 1978. Also see first-hand report on Chilean agrarian and food situation by the Institute for Food and Development Policy to be published in July 1979.

70. "Bitter Fruits," Latin America and Empire Report, Vol. X, No. 7, September, 1976, p. 21. North American Congress on Latin America, P. O.

Box 57, Cathedral Station, New York, NY 10025.

71. Cynthia Arnson and William Goodfellow, *OPIC: Insuring the Status Quo, International Policy Report,* Washington, D. C. : Center for International Policy, September, 1977, p. 3.

72. Latin American Agribusiness Development Corporation, Annual Reports, 1974, 1975, 1976, 1977 and 1978.

73. *CIC Brief,* October 1975, The Corporate Information Center of the Interfaith Center on Corporate Responsibility, Room 566, 475 Riverside Dr., New York, NY 10027.

74. David Wurfel, University of Windsor, Canada, "Philippine Agrarian Policy Today: Implementation and Political Impact," mimeo, 1977. Wurfel points out that the increase in the world price of sugar also contributed to the sugar expansion.

75. "Brazil Neglects Rural Labor and Land — World Bank," *Latin America Economic Report,* Vol. V. , No. 42, October 28, 1977, p. 192.

76. *Agricultural Development and Employment Performance: A Comparative Analysis,* Agricultural Planning Studies, No. 18, Food and Agriculture Organization, Rome, 1974.

77. Edgar Owens and Robert Shaw, *Development Reconsidered: Bridging the Gap Between Government and People,* Lexington, Mass: D. C. Heath, 1972, p. 60 and the World Bank, *Assault on World Poverty,* Baltimore: Johns Hopkins University Press, 1975, 215.

78. Kathleen Gough, "The 'Green Revolution' in South India and North Vietnam," *Social Scientist,* Kerala, India, August, 1977, No. 61 and for documentation of the drain of wealth by the elite in pre-revolutionary China see Leon Stover, *The Cultural Ecology of Chinese Civilization, Peasants* and *Elites in the Last of the Agrarian States,* New York; New American Library, 1974.

79. Walter Goldschmidt, *As You Sow: Three Studies in the Social Consequences of Agribusiness,* Montclair, N. J. : Allanheld, Osmun and Co., 1978.

80. Betsy Hartmann and James Boyce, *Needless Hunger: Voices from a Bangladesh Village.* See No. 16.

81. F. Tomasson Jannuzi and James T. Peach, Report on the Hierarchy of Interests in Land in Bangladesh, Washington D. C. : Agency for International Development, September, 1977, p. 75.

82. Frances Moore Lappé interview in Nashville, Tennessee, Jan. 15, 1979.

83. William Brune, State Conservationist, Soil Conservation Service, Des Moines, Iowa, testimony before Senate Committee on Agriculture and

Forestry, July 6, 1976; see also Seth King, "Iowa Rain and Wind Deplete Farmlands," *New York Times*, December 5, 1976, p. 61.

84. Kathleen Gough, "The 'Green Revolution' in South India and North Vietnam," *Social Scientist*, Kerala India, August, 1977. See also: Gough, *Ten Times More Beautiful*, New York: Monthly Review Press, 1978.

85. Calculations based on Food and Agriculture Organization, *Production Yearbooks*.

86. Calculated from Food and Agriculture Organization, *Trade Yearbook*, Vol. 29, 1975.

87. *Dietary Levels of Households in the United States*, Agricultural Research Service, USDA 17-17, 1968 and *First Health and Nutrition Examination Survey*, Preliminary Findings, Public Health Service, Health Resources Administration, U.S. Department of Health, Education and Welfare, Washington D. C. , 1972.

88. Corporate Data Exchange, Inc., *CDE Stock Ownership Directory No. 2, Agribusiness*, New York, 1979, p. 25, Table III.

89. A major project at the Institute for Food and Development Policy is the Food Security Project studying the successes and difficulties of the food systems in China, Mozambique, Cuba, Guinea Bissau, Vietnam, Somalia, Laos, Tanzania, the Soviet Union, and the countries of Eastern Europe.

90. *Learning from China*, A Report on Agriculture and the Chinese People's Communes by an FAO Study Mission, 1977, Regional Office for Asia and the Far East, FAO, Bangkok, Thailand and "China: The Great Exception," in *Poverty and Landlessness in Rural Asia*, Keith Griffin and Azizur Khan, eds., International Labour Office, Geneva, 1978.

91. Arthur MacEwan, *Agriculture and Development in Cuba*, manuscript prepared for the International Labor Organization, 1978.

92. Latin America Working Group (LAWG) Letter, Toronto, Canada Vol. 2, 7, Feb/March, 1975: 18-19.

93. Joseph B. W. Kuitenbrouwer, *Self-Reliance Without Poverty*, U. N. Economic and Social Commission for Asia and the Pacific, Bangkok, Thailand, 1976, p. 45.

94. Agency for International Development, *Congressional Presentation Fiscal Year 1979*, Main Volume, Washington, D.C., 1978, p. 139G-139I; and Michael Klare *Supplying Repression: U. S. Support for Authoritarian Regimes Abroad*. Institute for Policy Studies, 1977, p. 39.

95. Keith Dalton, "The Undernourished Philippines," *Far Eastern Economic Review,* September 1, 1978, p. 35, citing the Asian Development Bank and a 1977 report by the United Nations Protein-Calorie Advisory Group.

96. Agency for International Development, *Congressional Presentation Fiscal Year 1979, Main Volume,* Washington, D. C. , 1978, p. 23-27, 101-103, 139T-139X.

97. Center for International Policy, *Human Rights and the U. S. Foreign Assistance Program: FY 1978,* Part I-Latin America, Washington, D. C. , 1978.

98. Useful background reading on the International Monetary Fund is Cheryl Payer, *The Debt Trap: The IMF and the Third World,* London: Penguin Books, 1974.

99. World Bank, *World Development Report, 1978,* Washington D. C. , 1978, Table I, p. 76-77.

100. World Bank, *Annual Report, 1978,* Washington, D. C. , p. 26-27.

101. "India: Plenty of Cash, Food—Still in Need," *Los Angeles Times,* March 26, 1978, p. 9.

102. *Wall Street Journal,* June 14, 1978.

103. "Brazil Neglects Rural Labour and Land—World Bank," *Latin America Economic Report.* 28 October, 1977, p. 192, and notes of interview with Bishop Jose Rodriquez de Souza by representatives of Misereor (Geneva Catholic Relief Fund) September 1, 1978.

104. Milton J. Esman, *Landlessness and Near Landlessness* in Developing Countries, Ithaca: Center for International Studies, Cornell University, 1978.

105. *Ibid.* For further documentation see *Food First* (paperback) Part IX, Ballantine Books, New York, 1979.

106. Comptroller General of the United States, *Credit Programs for Small Farmers in Latin America Can Be Improved,* Report to Congress, Washington D.C., December 7, 1977.

107. FAO/World Bank Cooperative Program, *Draft Report of the Guatemala Agricultural Credit Project Preparation Mission,* Vol. 1, Main Text, Report No. 6/77 No. 5, March 4, 1977.

108. "The Nicaraguan AID Program: Rural Development Loan—INVIERNO," Washington Office of Latin America, Washington, D.C., May, 1977, citing "An Evaluation of AID Loan 524-T-031, INVIERNO," ATAK, October, 1976 and "INVIERNO, A Case Study,"

INCAE (Harvard Affiliated Business School), Managua, Nicaragua, 1977 and interviews with Nicaraguan government officials.

109. Per-Arne Stroberg, *Water and Development: Organizational Aspects of a Tubewell Irrigation Project in Bangladesh*, Swedish International Development Authority: Dacca, March, 1977.

110. Kay McCarthy, "World Neighbors Says Guatemalans Oppose Aid Plan," *The Oklahoma Journal*, August 30, 1978, p. 5.

111. U. S. General Accounting Office, *Disincentives to Agricultural Production in Developing Countries*, Report to Congress, Nov. 26, 1975, Washington D. C. , p. 25.

112. Cited in *Far Eastern Economic Review*, May 19, 1978, p. 35.

113. Wahidul Haque, et. al., *An approach to Micro-Level Development: Designing and Evaluation of Rural Development Projects*, U. N. Asian Development Institute, February, 1977, p. 15.

114. Lasse and Lisa Berg, *Face to Face*, Berkeley: Ramparts Press, 1971, p. 154.

Selected Sources

For a more complete source of readings and documentation see *Food First Resource Guide: Documentation on the Roots of World Hunger and Rural Poverty*, San Francisco, CA.: Institute for Food and Development Policy, 1979.

Agriculture/Population Statistics:

United Nations Food and Agriculture Organization, *Production Yearbooks* and *Trade Yearbooks.*

United States Department of Agriculture (USDA), *Handbook of Agricultural Charts*, 1975, 1976, 1977.

Our Land and Water Resources, USDA, Economic Research Service, May, 1974.

Impact of the Green Revolution "Production" Strategy:

See Part IV of the authors' book, *Food First*, Ballantine edition, 1979.

Griffin, Keith, *Land Concentration and Rural Poverty.* New York: Macmillan, 1976.

Griffin, Keith, *The Political Economy of Agrarian Change.* Cambridge, Mass: Harvard University Press, 1974.

Griffin, Keith, and Khan, Azizur Rahman, eds., *Poverty and Landlessness in Rural Asia*, A Study by the World Employment Programme, International Labor Office, Geneva, 1977.

Hewitt de Alcántara, Cynthia, *Modernizing Mexican Agriculture: Socioeconomic Implications of Technological Change*, Report No. 76.5, United Nations Research Institute for Social Development, Geneva, 1976.

The Social and Economic Implications of Large-Scale Introduction of New Varieties of Food-grain: Summary of Conclusions, Report No. 74.1, United Nations Institute for Social Development, 1974. (The authors have relied also upon data contained in the numerous country studies included in this study.)

Palmer, Ingrid, *The New Rice in Asia: Conclusions from Four Country Studies,*

United Nations Research Institute for Social Development, Geneva, 1976.

Perelman, Michael, *Farming for Profit in a Hungry World: Capital and the Crisis in Agriculture*, Montclair, New Jersey: Allanheld, Osmun & Co., 1977.

Internationalization of Food Control:

See Part VIII of the authors' book, *Food First*, Ballantine edition, 1979.

Barnet, Mueller, Ronald, *Global Reach: The Power of the Multinational Corporations*. New York: Simon and Schuster, 1974.

George, Susan, *How the Other Half Dies*. Montclair, New Jersey: Allanheld, Osmun & Co., 1976.

Ledogar, Robert J., *Hungry For Profits*. New York: IDOC, 1976.

The Agribusiness Manual, Interfaith Center on Corporate Responsibility, 475 Riverside Drive, New York, 10027.

Concentration of Control in the U.S. Food System:

See Part VII of the authors' book, *Food First*, Ballantine edition, 1979.

Belden, Joe, with Forte, Gregg, *Toward a National Food Policy*, Exploratory Project for Economic Alternatives, 1519 Connecticut Ave. NW, Washington, D.C. 20036.

Goldschmidt, Walter, *As You Sow: Three Studies in the Social Consequences of Agribusiness*. Montclair, New Jersey: Allanheld, Osmun & Co., 1978.

Hightower, Jim, *Eat Your Heart Out: How Food Profiteers Victimize the Consumer*. New York: Crown, 1975.

Public Policy and the Changing Structure of American Agriculture, Congressional Budget Office, September, 1978.

Fellmeth, Robert C., *Politics of Land: Ralph Nader's Study Group on Land Use in California*. New York: Grossman, 1973.

Marion, Mueller, Cotterill, Geithman, Schmelzer, *The Profit and Price Performance of Leading Food Chains*, 1970-74. Joint Economic Committee, April 12, 1977.

Conner, John M. and Mather, Loys L., *Directory of the 200 Largest U.S. Food and Tobacco Processing Firms*, 1975, Jointly published by Economics,

Statistics and Cooperatives Service, U.S.D.A. and the North Central Regional Project, July 1978.

The Relationship of U.S. Economic, Military, and Aid Policies to World Hunger:

See Part IX of the authors' book, *Food First*, Ballantine edition, 1979.

General Accounting Office, *Disincentives to Agricultural Production in Developing Countries*, Report to the Congress, 1975.

Center for International Policy, *Human Rights and the U.S. Foreign Assistance Program FY 1978*, Parts I, II, Washington, D.C., 1978.

Hartmann, Betsy and Boyce, James, *Needless Hunger: Voices from a Bangladesh Village*, Institute for Food and Development Policy, San Francisco, California, 1979.

Payer, Cheryl, *The Debt Trap: The IMF and the Third World*. Penguin Books, 1974.

Morrell, James, "Foreign Aid End Run Around Congress," Center for International Policy, Washington D.C., 1977.

Agency for International Development, Congressional Presentation, FY 1979, Main Volume.

The Inefficiencies of Concentrated Economic Control and the Productive Potential of Agrarian Reform:

See Part V of the authors' book, *Food First*, Ballantine edition, 1979.

Owens, Edgar and Shaw, Robert, *Development Reconsidered: Bridging the Gap Between Government and People*. Lexington, Mass., 1972.

Bergmann, Theodor, *Farm Policies in Socialist Countries*. Lexington, Mass: D.C. Heath & Co., 1975.

Henle, H.V., *Report on China's Agriculture*, Food and Agriculture Organization of the United Nations, Rome, 1975.

Jacoby, Erich, *The Green Revolution in China*. United Nations Research Institute for Social Development, Geneva, 1974.

MacEwan, Arthur, *Agriculture and Development in Cuba*, forthcoming, International Labor Office, Geneva, 1979.

Food and Agriculture Organization, *Progress in Land Reform—Sixth Report*,

Rural Institutions Division, Rome, 1975.)

Gough, Kathleen, *Ten Times More Beautiful: Rebuilding the Republic of Vietnam.* New York: Monthly Review Press, 1978.

SELECTED PUBLICATIONS

Weeklies

1. *In These Times,* 1509 N. Milwaukee, Chicago, IL 60622
2. *Africa News,* P. O. Box 3851, Durham, NC 27702

Monthlies and Periodicals

1. *Mother Jones,* 625 3rd Street, San Francisco, CA 94107
2. *Dollars and Sense,* 324 Somerville Avenue, Somerville, MA 02143
3. *Multinational Monitor,* P. O. Box 19312, Washington, DC 20036
4. *NACLA Report,* 151 West 19th Street, New York, NY 10011
5. *Community Jobs,* 1704 R Street N. W. , Washington, DC 20009
6. *Nutrition Action,* Center for Science in the Public Interest, 1957 S Street N. W. , Washington, DC 20009
7. *Food Monitor,* P. O. Box 1975, Garden City, NY 11530
8. *Catholic Rural Life,* 3801 Grand Avenue, Des Moines, IA 50312
9. *Monthly Review,* 116 West 14th Street, New York, NY 10011

Underdevelopment and World Hunger

1. Barnet, Richard J. and Muller, Ronald E. , *Global Reach: The Power of the Multinational Corporations* (Simon and Schuster: New York, 1974).
2. Beckford, George L. , *Persistent Poverty: Underdevelopment in Plantation Economies in the Third World* (Oxford University Press: New York, 1972).
3. Burbach, Roger and Flynn, Patricia, *Agribusiness in the Americas* (Monthly Review Press: New York, 1980).
4. Edwards, Reich, and Weisskopf, eds., *The Capitalist System* Harvard University Press: Cambridge, 1972).
5. George, Susan, *How the Other Half Dies* (Penguin Books: London, 1976).
6. Griffin, Keith, *The Political Economy of Agrarian Change* (Harvard University Press: Cambridge, 1974).
7. Gunder, Frank Andre, *Capitalism and Underdevelopment in Latin America* (Monthly Review Press: New York, 1967).

66

8. Gussow, Joan, ed., *The Feeding Web: issues in nutritional ecology* (Bull Publishing Co.: Palo Alto, CA, 1978).
9. Ledogar, Robert, *Hungry for Profits* (IDOC: New York, 1976).
10. Nelson, Jack A., *Hunger for Justice: The Politics of Food and Faith* (Orbis Books: Maryknoll, NY, 1980).
11. Perelman, Michael, *Farming for Profit in a Hungry World; Capital and the Crisis in Agriculture* (Land-Mark Studies, Universe Books: New York, 1977).
12. Rodney, Walter, *How Europe Underdeveloped Africa* (L'Ouverture Publications: London, 1972).
13. Sweezy, Paul, *Monopoly Capitalism* (Monthly Review Press: New York, 1970).
14. Williams, Eric, *Capitalism and Slavery* (Putnam: New York, 1966).

North American Agriculture and Food Policies

1. Fellmeth, Robert C., *Politics of Land* (Grossman Publishers: New York, 1933).
2. Freundlich, Collins, Wenig, eds., *A Guide to Cooperative Alternatives* (Community Publications Cooperative: New Haven, CT, 1979).
3. Hightower, Jim, *Eat Your Heart Out* (Vintage Books: New York, 1975).
4. Merrill, Richard, ed., *Radical Agriculture* (Harper Colophon Books: New York, 1976).
5. Morgan, Dan, *Merchants of Grain* (Viking: New York, 1979).
6. Rodefeld, Richard, ed., et al., *Change in Rural America* (The C. V. Mosby Co.: St. Louis, 1978).
7. Williams, Carey, *Factories in the Field* (Peregrine Press: Santa Barbara, CA, 1971).
8. Warnock, John, *Profit Hungry: The Food Industry in Canada* (New Star Books: Vancouver, BC, 1978).

SELECTED TRAINING ORGANIZATIONS

1. *Movement for a New Society*, 4722 Baltimore Avenue, Philadelphia, PA 19143
2. *Midwest Academy*, 600 Fullerton Avenue, Chicago, IL 60606
3. *New School for Democratic Management*, 589 Howard Street, San Francisco, CA 94105

SELECTED ACTION GROUPS

U. S. Agricultural Policies

1. Agribusiness Accountability Publications, 3410 19th Street, San Francisco, CA 94110, 415/665-6970. Publications: *AgBiz Tiller* (periodical); *Major U. S. Corporations Involved in Agribusiness* (1978 edition); *The Agribusiness Accountability Project Reader; The Fields Have Turned Brown* (Susan DeMarco and Susan Sechler); clipping service.
2. American Agricultural Movement, P. O. Box 57, Springfield, CO 81073, 302/523-6223. Publication: *American Agricultural News*.
3. American Agricultural Women, 6690 Walker Avenue N. W., Grand Rapids, MI 49504.
4. Center for Rural Affairs, P. O. Box 405, Walthill, NB 68087, 402/846-5428. Publications: *New Land Review* (newsletter) and research studies.
5. Consumers Opposed to Inflation in the Necessities (COIN), 2000 P Street N. W., Washington, DC 20036, 202/659-0800.
6. Emergency Land Fund, 836 Beecher Street S. W., Atlanta, GA 30310.
7. Exploratory Project for Economic Alternatives, Suite 515, 2000 P Street N. W., Washington, DC 20036, 202/833-3208.

8. Frank Porter Graham Center, Route 3, Box 95, Wadesboro, NC 28170.
9. National Catholic Rural Life Conference, 4625 N. W. Beaver Drive, Des Moines, IA 50322, 515/270-2634.
10. National Family Farm Coalition, Suite 624, 815 15th Street N. W., Washington, DC 20005, 202/638-4254.
11. National Farmers Organization, Corning, IA 50841. Publication: *The NFO Reporter.*
12. National Farmers Union, 1012 14th Street N. W., Washington, DC 20005, 202/628-9774. Publication: *Washington Newsletter.*
13. National Land for People, 2348 North Cornelia, Fresno, CA 93711, 209/233-4727. Publications: *People, Land, Food* (monthly); *Who Owns the Land* (monograph); slide show available.
14. Rural America, 1346 Connecticut Avenue N. W., Washington, DC 20036.
15. U. S. Farmers Association, P. O. Box 496, Hampton, IA 50441.

Direct Farmer-Consumer Marketing

1. Agricultural Marketing Project, Center for Health Services, 2606 Westwood Drive, Nashville, TN 37204.
2. Earthwork — Center for Rural Studies, 3410 19th Street, San Francisco, CA 94110, 415/626-1266. Publications: A complete directory of books and films on food and land.
3. Pike Place Market, 84 Pine Street, Seattle, WA 98101.

Alternative Food Systems

1. Arizona/New Mexico Federation of Co-ops, Albuquerque Outpost, 106 Girard S. E., Albuquerque, NM 87106, 505/265-7416.
2. CC Grains Collective Warehouse, 4501 Shilshole Avenue N. W., Seattle, WA 98107
3. Chicago Loop College, Food Co-op Project, 64 East Lake Street, Chicago, IL 60601.
4. Co-op Federation of Greater New York, Richard Parsekian, 378 Pacific, Brooklyn, NY 11217.
5. DANCE, 1401 South 5th Street, Minneapolis, MN 55454.
6. Earthwork (See No. 2, *Direct Farmer-Consumer Marketing*).
7. Federation of Ohio River Co-ops, 320-D Outerbelt Street, Columbus, OH 43213, 614/861-2446. Publication: *The Lovin' FORCfull*, 723 College Avenue, Morgantown, WV 26505.
8. Federation of Southern Cooperatives, P. O. Box 95, Epes, AL 35460.
9. Leon County Food Co-op Warehouse, 649 West Gaines Street, Tallahassee, FL 32304, 904/222-9916.
10. NEFCO, 8 Ashford, Allston, MA 02134, 617/A-Living.

Building Alliances — Farmer, Food Worker, Consumer

1. Consumers Federation, 5516 South Cornell, Chicago, IL 60637. Contact: Dan McCurry.
2. Earthwork (see No. 2, *Direct Farmer-Consumer Marketing*).
3. Coordinating Committee on Pesticides, Suite 106, 1057 Solano Avenue, Albany, CA 94706, 415/526-7141.

Local and Regional Focus

1. California Food Policy Coalition, 1300 North Street, Sacramento, CA 95814.
2. Center for Farm and Food Research, Inc., P. O. Box 166, Cornwall Bridge, CT 06754.

3. Center for Studies in Food Self-Sufficiency, Vermont Institute of Community Involvement, 90 Main Street, Burlington, VT 05401.
4. Coalition for Alternative Agriculture and Self-Sufficiency, c/o SCER, Campus Center Box 18, University of Massachusetts, Amherst, MA 01003, 413/545-2892.
5. Conference on Alternative State and Local Public Policy, 1901 Q Street N. W., Washington, DC 20009.
6. Coordinating Committee on Pesticides (see No. 3, *Building Alliances — Farmer, Food Worker, Consumer*).
7. Frank Porter Graham Center (see No. 8, *U. S. Agricultural Policies*).
8. Institute for Community Economics, Inc., 639 Massachusetts Avenue, Cambridge, MA 02139, 617/542-1060. Publication: *Community Land Trusts.*
9. Institute for Local Self-Reliance, 1717 18th Street N. W., Washington, DC 20009, 202/232-4108. Publication: *Self-Reliance.*
10. Rural Resources, R. R. 1, Box 11, Loveland, OH 45140, 513/683-9483.

Problems of Farmworkers and Food Workers

1. California Agrarian Action Project, P. O. Box 464, Davis, CA 95616, 916/756-8518. Publications: newsletter; pamphlet and slide show, "No Hands Touch the Land."
2. Farm Labor Organizing Committee (FLOC), 714½ South St. Clair Street, Toledo, OH 43609, 419/243-3456.
3. Northwest Seasonal Workers Association, 145 N. Oakdale Street, Medford, OR 97501, 503/773-6811.
4. United Farmworkers (AFL-CIO), P. O. Box 62, Keene, CA 93531, 805/822-5571.

Agricultural Research: Critiques and Alternatives

1. California Agrarian Action Project (see No. 1, *Problems of Farmworkers and Food Workers*).
2. Center for the Biology of Natural Systems, Box 1126, Washington University, St. Louis, MO 63130, 314/863-4812.
3. Institute for Local Self-Reliance (see No. 9, *Local and Regional Focus*).

Nutritional Decline, Government Food Programs, and Corporate Penetration of Institutional Food Systems

1. Center for Science in the Public Interest, 1757 S Street N. W., Washington, DC 20009, 202/332-9110. Publication: *Nutrition Action.*
2. Children's Foundation, Suite 1112, 1082 Connecticut Avenue N. W., Washington, DC 20036, 202/296-4451.
3. Community Nutrition Institute, 1910 K Street N. W., Washington, DC 20006, 202/833-1730.
4. Food Research and Action Center (FRAC), 2011 I Street N. W., Washington, DC 20006, 202/452-8250.
5. Mississippi Hunger Coalition, 406 Guidici Street, Jackson, MS 39204, 601/948-3672.

The Media and Food/Hunger

1. Action for Children's Television, 46 Austin Street, Newtonville, MA 02160, 617/527-7870.
2. Food Media Center, c/o Earthwork (see No. 2, *Direct Farmer-Consumer Marketing*).
3. World Hunger Year (W. H. Y.), P. O. Box 1975, Garden City, NY 11530, 516/742-3700. Organizes educational "radiothons" on hunger issues. Publication: *Food Monitor.* See also W. H. Y. of New Jersey, 27-06 High Street, Fairlawn, NJ 07410, 201/791-3828. Publication: *A Guide for Action on Food and Hunger in School and Community.*

Development, Trade, and Government Aid

1. Boston Industrial Mission, 56 Boylston Street, Cambridge, MA 02138, 617/491-6350. Publications: *Vectors; Women and Hunger.*
2. Bread for the World, 32 Union Square East, New York, NY 10003, 212/260-7005. Publication: newsletter, Christian Citizen's lobby on hunger issues.
3. Center of Concern, 3700 13th Street N. E. , Washington, DC 20017, 202/635-2757. Publication: *Center Focus.*
4. Center for Community Change, 1000 Wisconsin Avenue N. W. , Washington, DC 20007, 202/338-6310.
5. Center for Development Policy, 401 C Street N. E. , Washington, DC 20002, 202/547-1656.
6. Center for International Policy, 120 Maryland Avenue N. E. , Washington, DC 20002, 202/544-4666.
7. Clergy and Laity Concerned, 198 Broadway, New York, NY 10038, 212/964-6730.
8. Development Group for Alternative Policies, Suite 206, 2200 19th Street N. W. , Washington, DC 20009, 202/332-1600.
9. Food Policy Center, 538 7th Street S. E. , Washington, DC 20003, 202/547-7070.
10. Friends Committee on National Legislation, 245 2nd Street N. E. , Washington, DC 20002, 202/547-4343. Publication: *Washington Newsletter.*
11. Institute for Food and Development Policy, 2588 Mission Street, San Francisco, CA 94110, 415/648-6090. Publications: see enclosed publications catalogue.
12. Institute for Policy Studies, Transnational Institute, 1901 Q Street N. W. , Washington, DC 20009, 202/234-9382.
13. Interreligious Taskforce on U. S. Food Policy, 110 Maryland Avenue N. E. , Washington, DC 20002, 800/424-7292 (toll free). Publication: *Impact.*
14. Network, Suite 605, 1029 Vermont Avenue N. W. , Washington, DC 20005, 202/347-6200. Publication: newsletter.

U. S. Corporate Penetration in the Third World

1. Corporate Accountability Research Group, P. O. Box 19312, Washington, DC 20036, 202/387-8030. Publication: *Multinational Monitor* (monthly).
2. Corporate Data Exchange, Suite 707, 198 Broadway, New York, NY 10038, 212/962-2980. Study of ownership of agribusiness corporations.
3. INFACT, The Newman Center, 1701 University Avenue S. E. , Minneapolis, MN 55414, 612/331-3437.
4. Interfaith Center for Corporate Responsibility, Suite 566, 475 Riverside Drive, New York, NY 10027, 212/870-2294. Film: *Bottle Babies* (see question 38).
5. North American Congress on Latin America (NACLA), 151 West 19th Street, 9th floor, New York, NY 10011. Publication: *NACLA Report.*
6. Northern California Interfaith Committee on Corporate Responsibility (NC-ICCR), 3410 19th Street, San Francisco, CA 94110, 415/863-8060.

Ending U. S. Government Economic and Military Support to Anti-Democratic Regimes

1. Anti-Martial Law Coalition (Philippines), 41-32 56th Street, Woodside, NY 11377.
2. Clergy and Laity Concerned (see No. 7, *Development, Trade, and Government Aid*).
3. Coalition for a New Foreign and Military Policy, 120 Maryland Avenue N. E. , Washington, DC 20002, 202/546-8400. Publications: *Legislative Update and Key Votes; Action Alerts.*
4. Friends of the Filipino People (FFP), 110 Maryland Avenue N. E. , Washington, DC 20002, 202/296-2707. Publications: monthly bulletin and action suggestions.
5. National Network in Solidarity with the Nicaraguan People, 1322 18th Street N. W. , Washington, DC 20036, 202/223-9279.

6. Non-Intervention in Chile (NICH) (national office), Suite 905, 151 West 19th Street, New York, NY 10011, 212/989-5695.

Direct Assistance to Self-Help Efforts Abroad

1. American Friends Service Committee (national office), 1501 Cherry Street, Philadelphia, PA 19102, 215/241-7000; 15 Rutherford Place, New York, NY 10003, 212/777-4600; 2160 Lake Street, San Francisco, CA 94121, 415/752-7766. Publication: *World Hunger Action Letter*. Slide Show: "Hamburger, U. S. A." (agribusiness control over food system).
2. Economic Development Bureau, 234 Colony Road, New Haven, CT 06511, 203/776-9084. An alternative to corporate consulting services, the EDB puts people with technical skills in touch with progressive Third World groups.
3. Oxfam-America, 302 Columbus Avenue, Boston, MA 02116, 617/247-3304. Sponsors self-help projects domestically and in the Third World.
4. Unitarian Universalist Service Committee, Inc., 78 Beacon Street, Boston, MA 02108, 617/742-2120. Publication: A hunger action study kit.
5. Mennonite Central Committee (international and U. S. headquarters), 21 South 12th Street, Akron, PA 17501.

Other Organizations

1. Public Interest Research Group (PIRG), U. S. (a regional network), National Clearinghouse, 1329 E Street N. W. , Washington, DC 20004, 202/347-3811. Publication: newsletter. Multi-issue clearinghouse for student-funded research.
2. Public Resource Center, 1747 Connecticut Avenue N. W. , Washington, DC 20009. Publication: *The Elements*.

Canadian Organizations

1. Canadian Council for International Cooperation (national office), 75 Sparks Street, Ottawa, Ontario KlP 5A5, 613/235-4331.
2. Development Education Center, 121 Avenue Road, Toronto, Ontario.
3. DEVERIC, 1539 Birmingham Street, Halifax, Nova Scotia, 902/422-8339.
4. GATT-fly (national), 11 Madison Avenue, Toronto, Ontario M5R 2S2, 416/912-4615.
5. IDEA Center, Box 32, Station C, Winnipeg, Manitoba R3M 3S3.
6. IDERA, 2524 Cypress Avenue, Vancouver, British Columbia, 602/732-1214.
7. National Farmer's Union (national), 250 C 2nd Avenue, Saskatoon, Saskatchewan S7K 2M1, 306/652-9465.
8. One Sky Center, 134 Avenue F South, Saskatoon, Saskatchewan S7M 1S8, 306/652-1571.
9. Ontario Public Interest Research Group (OPIRG), 226 Physics Building, University of Waterloo, Waterloo, Ontario.
10. People's Food Commission (national office), 4th floor, 75 Sparks Street, Ottawa, Ontario K1P 5A5. Publication: newsletter. A cross-Canada inquiry into the food system in communities.

SELECTED AUDIOVISUALS

1. "Agribusiness Goes Bananas" slideshow. Earthwork-Center for Rural Studies (see No. 2, *Direct Farmer-Consumer Marketing*)
2. "Food First" slideshow or filmstrip. Institute for Food and Development Policy (see No. 11, *Development, Trade, and Government Aid*)
3. "Hamburger U. S. A." slideshow. American Friends Service Committee, San Francisco (see No. 1, *Direct Assistance to Self-Help Efforts Abroad*)

About the Institute . . .

The Institute for Food and Development Policy is a not-for-profit research, documentation and education center. It focuses on food and agriculture, always asking: Why hunger in a world of plenty?

By working to identify the root causes of hunger and food problems here and abroad, the Institute provides counter messages:

- No country in the world is a hopeless "basket case."
- The illusion of scarcity is a product of the unequal control over food-producing resources; inequality in control over these resources results in their underuse and misuse.
- The hungry are not our enemies. Rather, we and they are victims of the same economic forces which are undercutting their food security us well as ours.

The staff of the Institute: Frances Moore Lappé and Joseph Collins, co-founders, David Kinley, Bruce Randall, Patty Somlo, Douglas Basinger, Judy Post, Rodney Freeland, Chris Anderegg, and Luanne Rowder.

For more information write to the Institute for Food and Development Policy, 2588 Mission Street, San Francisco, CA 94110 U. S. A.

Financial Support

The Institute solicits contributions from individuals, church groups, and private foundations. In addition, monies are received through speaking engagements and literature sales. The Institute does not accept funding from governments or corporations.

More and more, the Institute depends on individual donors, literature sales and speaking engagements. In addition, we are grateful for current contributions from the Arca Foundation, Columbia Foundation, Ottinger Foundation, Samuel Rubin Foundation, Shalan Foundation, Stern Fund, Tides Foundation, The Youth Project, Church of the Brethren, Episcopal Church, Maryknoll Fathers, United Methodist Church, United Presbyterian Church, First United Church (Oak Park, Illinois), and St. James Episcopal Church (New York).

Friends of the Institute

Because the Institute's work threatens many established interests, we believe that our effectiveness depends on developing the widest possible base of support. By joining the Friends of the Institute program you can receive our expanding list of publications at a generous discount or free.

All contributors of $25 or more receive a free copy of the paperback edition of the highly acclaimed *Food First: Beyond the Myth of Scarcity* by Frances Moore Lappé and Joseph Collins, with Cary Fowler (Ballantine, 1979). Contributors of $100 or more also receive one free copy of all major Institute publications for one year. Contributors of $25 or more also receive a 50 percent discount on one copy of all Institute publications for one year.

All contributions are tax-deductible.

Institute Publications

El Hambre en el Mundo: Diez Mitos, a Spanish-language version of *World Hunger: Ten Myths* plus additional information about food and agriculture policies in Mexico. 72 pages. **$1.45**

Food First: Beyond the Myth of Scarcity, 50 questions and responses about the causes and proposed remedies for world hunger. Frances Moore Lappé and Joseph Collins, with Cary Fowler 620 pages, Ballantine Books, revised 1979. **$2.75**

Food First Resource Guide, documentation on the roots of world hunger and rural poverty. Institute staff, 80 pages with photographs. **$2.95**

Needless Hunger: Voices from a Bangladesh Village exposes the often brutal political and economic roots of needless hunger. Betsy Hartmann and James Boyce, 72 pages with photographs. **$2.95**

What Can We Do? An action guide on food, land and hunger issues. Interviews with over one dozen North Americans involved in many aspects of these issues. William Valentine and Frances Moore Lappé, 60 pages with photographs. **$2.45**

Mozambique and Tanzania: Asking the Big Questions looks at the questions which face people working to build economic and political systems based on equity, participation and cooperation. Frances Moore Lappé and Adele Beccar-Varela, 128 pages with photographs. **$4.75**

Agrarian Reform and Counter-Reform in Chile, a firsthand look at some of the current economic policies in Chile and their effect on the rural majority. Joseph Collins, 24 pages with photographs. **$1.00**

Aid as Obstacle: Twenty Questions on our Foreign Aid and the Hungry critically analyzes U. S. -funded foreign assistance in a question and answer format. Frances Moore Lappé, Joseph Collins, David Kinley, 160 pages with photographs. **$4.95**

Aid to Bangladesh: For Better or Worse?, an interview showing the misuse of aid throughout Bangladesh. First of Impact Series with Oxfam-America. Michael Scott, 28 pages with photographs. **$1.45**

Reprint Packet No. 1, a compilation of eight articles by Institute staff which have appeared in a wide range of periodicals. 16 pages. **$1.45**

Research Reports. "Infant Formula Promotion and Use in the Philippines," Frances Moore Lappé and Eleanor McCallie. **$1.25**

"The Banana Industry in the Philippines: An Informal Report," Frances Moore Lappé and Eleanor McCallie. **$1.95**

Food First Slideshow/Filmstrip in a visually positive and powerful portrayal demonstrates that the cause of hunger is not scarcity but the increasing concentration of control over food-producing resources. 30 minutes.

$89 (slideshow), $34 (filmstrip)

Write for our free publications catalogue.
All publications orders must be prepaid.